Cartoon Workshop

How to create humour

Joel Mishon with Ed Beardwell

DEDICATION

To our respective parents and friends, and to the memory of Nicholas Newman.

Thanks to everyone at CartoonStock – Kelley for giving us time to get this done and Eleni, Marilyn and Zakia for occasionally turning up to work. Thanks also to John O'Brien and Bill Dale; to Cathy Gosling and Caroline Churton at HarperCollins; to Pedro and Frances Prá-Lopez at Kingfisher Design; to our editor Geraldine Christy; and to any friends and relations who, on seeing our names on the front of this book, buy it.

First published in 2003 by
Collins, an imprint of
HarperCollins*Publishers*
77-85 Fulham Palace Road
Hammersmith, London W6 8JB

The Collins website address is:
www.collins.co.uk

Collins is a registered trademark of HarperCollins Publishers Limited.

04 06 07 05 03
2 4 6 5 3 1

A catalogue record for this book is available from the British Library

Produced by Kingfisher Design, London
Editor: Geraldine Christy
Art Director: Pedro Prá-Lopez
Designer: Frances Prá-Lopez

Contributing artists:
All cartoons by Joel Mishon other than those listed below.
Joel Mishon *(pages 36 top left, 60, 61, © Private Eye)*

Arnaldo Almeida *(page 67)*, Angonoa *(pages 26, 72)*, Bruce Baillie *(page 68)*, Ian Baker *(pages 20 centre, 22, 32 centre right)*, Mike Baldwin *(pages 28, 40, 93 bottom)*, Isabella Bannerman *(pages 38, 46, 92)*, Stefano Baratti *(page 82)*, Paul Black (Fishhead) *(page 94)*, Adey Bryant *(pages 14 left, 31, 63)*, Shannon Burns *(page 88 bottom)*, Keith Clayton *(page 55)*, David Cooney *(page 70)*, Santiago Cornejo *(page 73)*, Andy Davey *(page 16)*, Dave Connaughton (Deacon) *(page 34)*, John Docherty (Jorodo) *(page 77)*, Pete Dredge *(page 50 top)*, Stan Eales *(page 79)*, Claudio Furnier *(page 53 top)*, Clive Goddard *(pages 12, 23, 29 bottom right, 35 top, 43)*, Grizelda *(page 90)*, Richard Jolley (RGJ) *(pages 15 top right, 35 bottom right, 44 top, 95 top)*, Anthony Kelly *(pages 15 top left, 87)*, Ham Khan *(pages 25, 91 top)*, Jerry King *(page 49)*, Peter King (PaK) *(pages 29, 66)*, Duncan McCoshan (Knife) *(pages 50 bottom, 86, 95 bottom)*, John McGillen *(page 65)*, Randy McIllwaine *(pages 69, 76)*, Andy McKay (Naf) *(pages 14 bottom right, 56 top, 75)*, Mark Milligan (Markie) *(pages 47 bottom, 62)*, David Myers *(page 71)*, Marc Tyler Nobleman *(page 74)*, Alan de la Nougerede *(page 32 left)*, Werner Wejp-Olsen *(page 53 bottom)*, Giles Pilbrow *(pages 19, 20 bottom left)*, Oliver Preston *(pages 52, 64, 78, 80)*, Dan Rosandich *(page 89)*, Michael Ryan (Moic) *(page 91 bottom)*, Kevin Smith (Kes) *(page 56 bottom)*, Mike Stokoe *(page 17)*, Ron Therien *(page 37)*, Robert Thompson *(pages 13, 44 bottom, 47 top, 88 top, 93 top)*, Mike Williams *(pages 41, 81, 83)*

ISBN 0 00 713801 6

Colour origination by Colourscan, Singapore
Printed in Scotland by Scotprint, Haddington

CONTENTS

INTRODUCTION

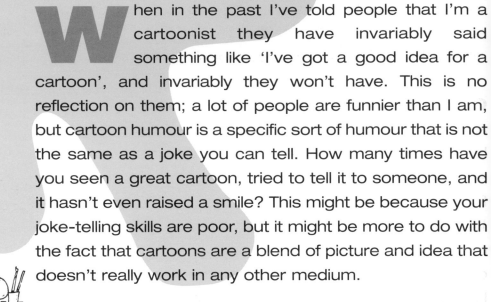

When in the past I've told people that I'm a cartoonist they have invariably said something like 'I've got a good idea for a cartoon', and invariably they won't have. This is no reflection on them; a lot of people are funnier than I am, but cartoon humour is a specific sort of humour that is not the same as a joke you can tell. How many times have you seen a great cartoon, tried to tell it to someone, and it hasn't even raised a smile? This might be because your joke-telling skills are poor, but it might be more to do with the fact that cartoons are a blend of picture and idea that doesn't really work in any other medium.

Why read this book?

This book has been written for anyone who enjoys cartoons and is interested in learning or honing their skills to create their own work. Many books have been written with the aim of teaching cartoon drawing (I recommend John Byrne's book *Learn to Draw Cartoons* published by HarperCollins), but few, if any, concentrate solely on creating the ideas behind cartoons or how you turn those ideas into something that others will find amusing.

The ideas and the drawing

Humour in cartoons is a mix of the ideas and the drawing. So this book is divided into two main sections. The first part concentrates on how cartoonists, and you, can invent ideas and jokes. The second focuses on how different drawing styles can illustrate and aid that humour to create professional cartoons. I've included exercises throughout that will allow you to develop your own skills and there's a cartoon showcase at the back showing you how different cartoonists can produce very different results from the same basic tools.

Cartoons – we've got 'em

As the cartoon editor at CartoonStock I get to see a large number of cartoons, and I am always interested in encouraging new talent, which was one of the reasons for writing this book in the first place. In *Cartoon Workshop* I have been able to use lots of cartoons by many of the world's best gag cartoonists to illustrate the different skills you will require to create your own work. I hope you will enjoy them as much as I do, and that you find the material funny as a collection of cartoons as well as an inspiration for your own creativity.

Most of this book has been written in the first person because it largely represents my personal view of how humour is created. However, I've been greatly helped by Ed Beardwell, who not only assisted me in choosing and interpreting the cartoons but also made sense (we hope) of the jumbled concepts I keep in my mind! His contribution has been invaluable in shaping the book as a whole, for which many thanks are due.

Enjoy the book and best of luck from us both!

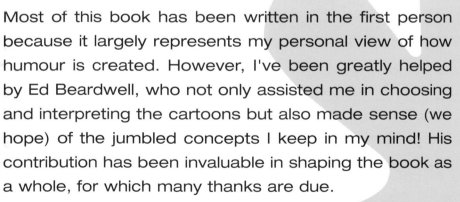

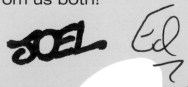

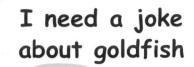

SECTION ONE

THE

I need a joke about goldfish

Okay, I'm waiting

Nope, no ideas so far

Maybe I'll make a cup of tea

I've got it ...
No, it's gon

Where to begin? Looking for ideas? *The Observer* cartoonist Ham Khan describes the process of cartooning as 'organized daydreaming'. That is a perfect description of what is required to come up with new cartoon ideas. Cartoonists don't just sit down and wait for inspiration to strike; they have processes to channel their thoughts and create jokes. This is what this section will explain.

Obviously all cartoonists work in different ways and there are numerous methods to reach a final result. Many cartoonists work intuitively and might

IDEAS

be unaware of the process they are using. This section, however, will explain a basic method for constructing jokes. It includes work on personal brainstorming, gets your brain working on lateral thinking and looks at the different types of joke that can make up a toolbox for creating your own humour. I'll talk you through some of the basic mental tools and templates for constructing new ideas, including work on puns, observation, satire and surreal concepts. I've discussed examples of each 'joke type' and there are exercises to practise each mental tool. Enjoy – and remember, I'll know if you haven't done the exercises.

How to come up with ideas

Before you can start drawing cartoons the first skill any cartoonist needs to develop is a method of stimulating his or her own imagination to come up with lots of different thoughts and ideas that can be built upon.

GETTING STARTED

If you've got a blank piece of paper in front of you it can be quite daunting. The temptation is to start drawing straightaway. Now I hate to sound boring or like your English teacher at school (unless they were particularly good), but you should really try and plan in advance. You can spend all day drawing funny faces and figures on your paper, but unless you have an idea first, it is very rare that your doodling will turn into a finished cartoon. Doodling can sometimes help the thought process, but you generally need to be a bit more systematic in your approach if you want to come up with a regular stream of ideas. Even if you haven't a single workable thought in your head it's good practice to keep pen on paper. If nothing else, it concentrates the mind and prevents it drifting off.

Cartoonist's tip

Though there are systematic methods to coax your brain into coming up with ideas, some ideas will just strike you from nowhere. It's always worth having a pen and pad with you to write down thoughts and doodles when they occur.

FUNNY DOODLES

GOOD IDEAS

Bouncing ideas off others

When you're chatting with your friends one person will say something, and that will remind someone else of something related. They will add their comment, that comment will provoke a thought from someone else and the conversation will develop. Within this conversation someone will invariably say something funny, normally induced by something someone else has said. It may be a pun, sarcasm or something silly, but the thought will have been stimulated by something someone else has said. In essence what is happening is that lots of ideas and thoughts are being created. They may not all be original, funny or, in some cases, even interesting but it is this process of a turnover of thoughts that you can replicate yourself to stimulate your imagination to find funny ideas.

Though the ideas and jokes you will hear in general conversation will not necessarily work for cartoon gags they will often spark your own thoughts. However, continual general conversation with friends is not really a very practical way of coming up with new ideas. Your friends may not want to play, and may not want to talk about what you need to create a joke about. That's where personal brainstorming and daydreaming come in, as we shall see …

Warning

As I mentioned in the Introduction, cartoon jokes are not the same as spoken jokes. They are a combination of drawing and idea. Things that make your friends laugh in conversation will not necessarily translate into cartoons, even if a similar thought process is at work.

BRAINSTORMING

Personal brainstorming or organized daydreaming is really a process to stimulate your own thoughts in the same way that ideas and thoughts come from a conversation. Obviously you have nobody to bounce ideas off when you work on your own cartoons, so you have to bounce ideas off yourself.

My method
My method for doing this is to take a blank piece of paper and write down a few topics that I think might be interesting. Once I've done that I start writing down other words or doodle ideas that I associate with the first headings or stimulate a tangential thought. For example, I might write down the word 'sheep'. The word sheep reminds me of 'Dolly' the sheep, the world's first cloned animal. When I start doodling sheep on the paper I realize that all sheep look the same to us anyway and the idea of cloning them begins to seem ridiculous, and now I have the germ of a funny idea.

Cartoonist's tip

Not every thought you have will be funny. The technique, therefore, is to keep going, turning over new thoughts and ideas until something that you think of makes you laugh. If it makes you laugh, it might make someone else laugh as well.

▶ On my worksheet (right) I started by writing down the words 'modern art' after a visit to the Tate. Underneath I wrote down associated thoughts and doodles till an idea began to form (ticked at bottom left).

ORGANIZED DAYDREAMING

To explain the process more fully I've taken my worksheet from the previous page and broken it down into a mini flow diagram (below) so that you can see how one idea led to another, until I had something that might work as a full cartoon.

Absorb information

Of course, even finding headings to go at the top of the page to start your imagination off can be difficult. Sometimes you may feel as if there is nothing in your head at all. You need concepts and observations so that you have something to brainstorm about. There are many ways you can stimulate your mind – by reading books and newspapers, watching TV, remembering conversations and noticing things during the rest of your day. This background information will not just give you your initial 'headers' for topics, but absorbing as much information as you can will also help when it comes to thinking around your initial topics and brainstorming.

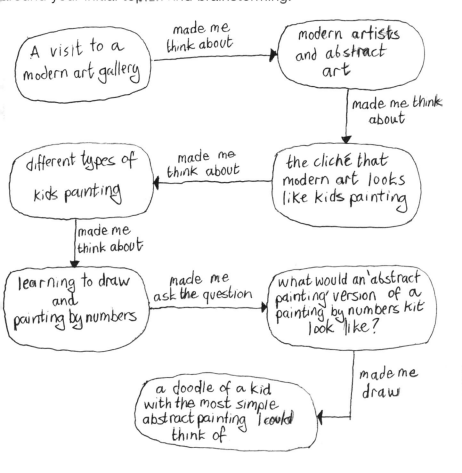

Warning

There will be times when you can think of nothing at all, however many tricks you use. This happens to everyone at some point. In this situation get up, have a walk around, distract yourself for a bit and try again. But don't use 'cartoonist's block' as an excuse all the time. If you want to be professional you have to work, whatever the problem.

◄ *Obviously with your own work you don't need to make flow diagrams, but this one serves to fill in the gaps not shown in my real, rather chaotic, working on the opposite page.*

SURPRISE

One thing that is essential to almost all cartoons is surprise. Surprise is essential to humour because it confounds the viewer's expectations and offers a fresh perspective. How many times have you heard or seen a bad joke that made you groan and said 'That's obvious, I saw that coming'? It can be assumed, therefore, that good jokes are the non-obvious. They are the unexpected laugh, a benign version of what makes you jump in a horror movie.

You may laugh because an idea is surreal, has hit a nerve, is childish, embarrassing or pokes fun at something important (all these areas are covered later in this book), but unless the joke is offered in a fresh take it may well not make anyone laugh.

CASE STUDY

Surprise can be created by something as simple as a pun. In Clive Goddard's cartoon there is a surprise awaiting the father, which creates humour for the viewer as outlined on page 13, but the cartoon wouldn't work if the real surprise did not lie with the surprising double meaning of 'mobile business'.

The humour here is created by:

a) *The pun that gives a surprising twist for the viewer and the father.*
b) *The drawing, which allows the viewer to see something that is hidden from the father.*

Clive Goddard

'Felicity tells me you run your own mobile business.'

'I'll have the squid surprise.'

We know something you don't

In drama there is a term called 'dramatic irony' that refers to an aspect in a play where the audience is aware of something that the character on stage is not. In a cartoon this same device can be used to create humour by letting the viewer become aware of something that will come as a surprise to the subject of the cartoon.

In Robert Thompson's cartoon above, therefore, there are two types of surprise that aid the humour. There is the surprise awaiting the customer, and we laugh in expectation of what may be about to happen to the unsuspecting man ordering his meal. The Germans have a word for this type of reaction – *Schadenfreude* (which means pleasure at others' misfortune). However, there is still another kind of 'surprise' for the viewer reading the cartoon because the whole scenario is unusual for the viewer. It is not something you would see in the real world. The literal translation of 'squid surprise' is as unlikely for the viewer as for the customer and therefore the viewer is likely to laugh at the unexpected.

◀ *Both Robert Thompson's and Clive Goddard's cartoons rely on the expression on the face of the 'victim' to be innocent and totally unaware of what is behind them.*

Cartoonist's tip

Though most cartoons will require surprise, they do not all require puns or 'dramatic irony'. Surprise is really the twist that makes an idea fresh for the viewer. The type of joke is as likely to be an observational or surreal one, as a pun.

JOKE TEMPLATES

Why do you think there are so many desert island jokes? The short answer is that even professional cartoonists need to use already created scenarios as a springboard for their imaginations sometimes. Cartoonists by their very nature will look at the work of others. If they find something funny by another artist they might take the same scenario and see if they can create another joke for it.

The desert island joke

The desert island joke as a scenario has developed a life of its own. The more it appears, the more artists remember it, and the more likely artists are to use it when inspiration fails to strike. The plight of being marooned on a desert island offers a scenario that tends to concentrate the mind. The situation has in-built comic potential. There is nowhere to go, there is nothing to do, and there is usually no-one to talk to. This contrasts so much with everyday life that any attempt at 'normal' behaviour will have a comic twist and the scenario can be used to comment on anything from holidays to recycling, as the two examples on this page demonstrate.

▼ (Below) *Adey Bryant has taken the idea of a message in a bottle to create a surreal notion of a bottle bank. It works because it is so incongruous on an island.*

▼ (Below right) *Andy McKay (Naf) has the same basic scenario, but has exaggerated the notion of a beach tide to achieve his cartoon.*

Adey Bryant

Andy McKay (Naf)

'It looks very different when the tide's out.'

'… You're once, twice, three times a lady …'

'Men! You're all alike!'

Other templates

In reality desert island jokes are such a cliché that editors tend not to use them unless they are a very different take on the old theme. There are, however, lots of other scenarios that cartoonists tend to use again and again, and you can use the same ideas as well to create your own cartoons. For instance, Noah's Ark, marriage counsellors and beggars with 'will work for …' signs are all seen much more often in cartoons than in the real world.

In the examples above both Anthony Kelly (left) and Richard Jolley (right) have seen the humour potential not just in the idea of cloning, but in having three people looking exactly the same. There is something instantly funny about clones because the sight is so unusual. We do not find the idea of sheep looking the same funny because to us they all do anyway. However, even though both artists have used the same scenario as a building block for the joke, their finished cartoons are very different.

Warning

Using common scenarios is not a licence to plagiarize. There is a real difference between using someone else's scenario and lifting a whole gag. It's worth remembering too that, though using standard scenarios works well sometimes, editors prefer totally new ideas and will quickly tire of an artist who only follows the herd, with no originality of his or her own.

Types of humour

There's no such thing as a new joke, just an old one wearing new clothes. Here I'll show you the main 'old jokes' and how you can use them for your own cartoons. If you do discover a new joke, don't touch it, but call me immediately ...

THE PUN

The pun is the simplest form of joke and the easiest one to explain. A pun is simply 'the humorous use of a word to create different meanings or a word or words with similar sounds but different meanings'. Puns are funny because they create images, ideas and associations that are unexpected and/or surprising.

Pun warning

Though puns are an essential part of humour, and most cartoonists will use them at one time or another you should be aware of certain points.

The fact that a word can have more than one meaning is not funny in itself. Most puns are obvious, they provide no element of surprise,

'My Bert's found God.'

Andy Davey

CASE STUDY

In this cartoon the humour comes not just from the wordplay but from how Andy Davey has interpreted his initial concept. Before he started the picture it had occurred to him that 'finding God' could have more than one meaning.

What makes this cartoon funny is:

a) *The idea that God is hiding under the stairs, an unexpected location.*
b) *The fact that He is embarrassed to be found, an unusual emotion for God.*
c) *The mild blasphemy (naughtiness) of making fun of an important subject.*
d) *The surprise of a stock phrase that is recognized to mean one thing and putting it in a different context.*

they do not lend themselves to interesting or unusual imagery and they have probably been heard before. Unless you have a fresh idea or an interesting take on an old idea the joke will not work.

Some editors hate puns. Though they can work, they are considered to be a very unsophisticated and easy form of wit and some editors will not buy them under any circumstance.

You can't translate puns into other languages. If you want your humour to travel well avoid puns at all costs.

Forty years man and wife and the chemistry was still there.

Building on the pun

In the cartoon above the artist has chosen to re-interpret a well-known phrase or cliché. He has taken what is essentially a metaphor and drawn a literal interpretation of it. The humour does not just come from the concept itself. In fact the pun is quite obvious, but once the artist has his initial idea he can create a drawing that is funny in itself. The surreal notion of an enormous chemical experiment taking place in the middle of a married couple's front room is entertaining even before we look at the caption. As with the God cartoon opposite, it is the drawing, its style and its various individual details that create the humour as much as the initial pun.

What makes the picture work are the expressions on the old couple's faces, showing that they are quite oblivious to the dangerous-looking piece of scientific equipment between them.

The Groan Factor

Most puns will only work if you are adding something else beyond just pointing out that a particular word or phrase can have more than one meaning. However, as everyone knows, some jokes can be so bad that they are actually good, simply because someone has had the cheek to use them! If the joke is so obvious, or the similarity between two words so tenuous, you can score a result by subverting the genre.

Joel Mishon

'The knights are drawing inn.'

Cartoon workout

Now that you have got the idea, here's your chance to work up some punning cartoons of your own. To get the ball rolling look at the sketches below showing you how I arrived at this final punning cartoon. Then get to work on the exercises on the right.

▲ When I sat down at my desk I saw my credit card bill and started to write down a few thoughts. I came up with a rhino charging pun and did a doodle.

▲ I liked my initial doodle of a rhino, now I needed a scenario. A rhino in a shop was surreal, but my punch line made the joke seem laboured.

'I don't like the way that rhino's preparing to charge!'

Now it's your turn!

1 Take these bad puns and stock phrases and turn them into a cartoon. Remember the joke should come as much from how you draw up the image as from the concept itself.

- **I'm handing in my notice**
- **They opened the door in their dressing gowns**
- **He's turning over a new leaf**

2 Think of five well-known phrases or sayings that can have more than one meaning, select the best one and draw up the unusual meaning into a cartoon.

3 'Death in Venice?' is the caption for a cartoon on page 29. Without looking at it draw up your own version and then compare the two.

◀ A safari scene seemed to work best in the end. I liked the surreal quality of placing a cash register in the wild.

OBSERVATIONAL HUMOUR

A lot of what makes us laugh is recognition of our own, or other people's, shortcomings. We laugh with relief and embarrassment when we realize that other people do the same things and have the same foibles and frustrations as ourselves. This is rich territory for cartoonists. If you can find an aspect of life that irritates, embarrasses or frustrates you, and depict it well, you are almost guaranteed to find an audience that has shared that experience. When they laugh it will be as much about a memory of their own or other people's misfortune as your clever idea. In many ways the humour works in a similar way to a true anecdote about yourself that you tell a friend.

CASE STUDY

Anyone who has been to a video store with a partner has probably argued over which film to take out. In this cartoon Giles Pilbrow has found a humorous way of illustrating this frustration by inventing a new category of 'unhappy compromise'.

The humour here works because:

a) Not only is a common experience identified but the notion invented that films could be categorized as viewers experience them.
b) The facial expressions remind the viewer of their own frustrations.

Giles Pilbrow

> 'Research and reading are the key to cartooning for me, not a blank piece of paper. Once you have your subject, or observation, half the battle's won.'
>
> Robert Thompson

Cartoonist's tip

It is the small things in life that generate the most humour. A lot of the appeal in a joke comes from depicting a common experience that nobody else has found worthy of comment before. Try to avoid what is obvious.

Observation is not about
noticing everything and
trying to make a joke
about it. It is about
reflecting on your own
experience. You don't have
to go out with a notepad to
notice that it's difficult to
open a carton of milk.

▼ *This is a perfect
observational cartoon.
Pilbrow again creates
humour in a common
experience by imagining
what shower controls
should say.*

Giles Pilbrow

Observation is not enough on its own

Simply identifying a common experience is not enough. You have to
twist or exaggerate the idea to increase its humour potential. Look at
the example below of the couple watching television. Noticing that
men can be lazy or that remote controls are useful doesn't make the
point. What the artist, Ian Baker, has done is to exaggerate both our
laziness and the bizarre lengths to which we will go to avoid standing
up and changing channels. As with all cartoons the humour comes
from both the drawing and the idea of a situation that probably rings
a bell with many a TV watcher. Would the caption be funny if the man
was standing up and changing channels in the normal way?

Ian Baker

'Why don't we just get a remote control?'

Know your audience

Some experiences are common to all, but all social groups will have
their own particular shared observations. This can be both an
advantage and a disadvantage. If, for example, you are a weasel
farmer and have some great observation to make about weasel
farming you may find that without the shared weasel experience not
everyone will get it. The joke may be fine if you intend selling it to
Weasel Magazine, but you may have to make the observation more
universal if you want to reach a wider and more general market.

Cartoon workout

Now all you have to do is reflect on your own experience and pull out the funny bits. In the example below my own experience was being nagged about not putting the bins out ...

▲ Initially I just doodled a scenario as it happened, but there was no actual humour in it, only a realization that men and women think differently.

▲ Then I tried to write down a list of differences between the sexes, but put them in an unusual context that would be both surprising and recognizable.

GENETIC INFORMATION MAPPING

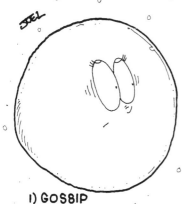

1) GOSSIP

2) EMOTIONAL MATURITY

3) DOING MORE THAN ONE THING AT ONCE

1) FOOTBALL STATISTICS

2) FIGHTING

3) GADGETS

4) FORGETTING TO PUT THE BINS OUT

1 Look at this list of modern frustrations and illustrate them. Note the smaller the frustration the more exaggerated the reaction can be.

- **Drink dispensers**
- **Computers crashing**
- **Seating on an economy-class flight**

2 Compare your idea for illustrating economy class with the one on page 31. Does your own work as well? How can you improve your version?

3 Look again at the video-shop joke on page 19. Redraw it in your own style, but with the caption 'something you both like'. How do the expressions change?

Finally I thought about genetic mapping. This seemed the perfect vehicle for what I wanted to convey.

WHAT IF ...?

If you are racking your brains and can't find anything funny in your own experience, don't worry. Why not imagine an unusual scenario and guess what might happen next?

Essentially you need to ask yourself questions such as what would happen if X met Y, or what would happen if Y went to Z. The factors do not have to be extreme, but in order to spark the imagination they should not normally be associated with each other. Of course, not all unusual situations will work well, but as you come up with more and more unlikely combinations one of them is likely to strike you as funny. If you think a scenario is funny it's a fair assumption that someone else will find it funny as well.

'It works a bit like David Bowie and his cut-up song lyrics. The juxtaposition of two different items can stimulate thought.'

Mike Williams

● Warning

Putting people in strange scenarios alone will not guarantee a good joke. A fox visiting the job centre is not funny in itself, but if he was looking for a vacancy at a chicken farm you might have something.

▶ *Notice how Ian Baker has used the eyes of his character to lead the viewer to see the dilemma that faces him.*

Ian Baker

IAN BAKER..

'You must be mature, spacious,
close to local amenities,
semi-detached,
and need attention.'

Clive Goddard

Estate Agent's date

Generating 'what if' scenarios

One way to generate 'what if' scenarios is to write down a list of random people, professions, places and things. Put two or three of them together and just see what happens. When I used to teach cartooning at the Cartoon Art Trust my colleague John Byrne came up with a class exercise of getting someone to draw a person, the next to draw an object and another to draw a location. The last person then had to combine all the elements into a full cartoon. I'm not saying all the results were successful, but the exercise resulted in some interesting ideas that could be honed later.

Look at the cartoon opposite. In this image Ian Baker has imagined a scenario of a skier in the men's toilets. The success of the cartoon relies as much on the skier's puzzlement at what to do in the situation as the situation itself. Note how Ian conveys perplexity by placing the skier's hand near his downturned mouth. Remember expression is not just about faces but the position of the whole body.

Cartoonist's tip

If your mind goes blank look through a dictionary, find a few random words and see what you can do with them. Looking through a magazine can also be a good kick-start to the imagination, but don't get too distracted.

Cartoon workout

As a simple example of a 'what if …' situation I've included a cartoon of what might happen if a sheep and a chicken were in a shoot-out. Although this is a single-panel cartoon there are really three scenes. The first two heighten the expectation of the viewer before the payoff. The scene would not work with just the third panel.

▲ When doodling I found I had drawn a sheep and a gunslinger. I began to wonder what a sheep gunslinger would do.

▲ I thought a sheep would run away, but the sheep needed something to react against that would heighten the humour.

READY....

STEADY....

GO!

Now it's your turn!

1 Imagine a cat was an exchange student at a school full of dogs. What would happen? How would you convey the humour to the viewer?

2 Draw up two different versions of the scene. Which works better?

3 Now look at the cartoon on page 37. Is the artist's idea similar to yours? Try and work out what makes Ron Therien's cartoon work well. Is yours as successful?

◀ Movement is important to this cartoon. If the two had just walked away the surprise and humour of the third picture would be lost. Would it work with two chickens?

SILENT HUMOUR

A silent cartoon is one that requires no caption and has no punch line. This type of cartoon can be created using many approaches, but for it to be successful you must have a concept that can be illustrated without words. However, one technique is unique for the creation of pure visual jokes – this is the visual pun.

The visual pun

A visual pun is where one thing looks like another when drawn. Cartoonists often find when they are doodling that one object can look similar to another. A schoolboy example of this would be the fact that when you draw one small circle in a larger circle it can be a target, a wheel or an aerial view of a Mexican wearing a hat.

CASE STUDY

In this cartoon by Ham Khan the visual pun is the similarity in shape between an igloo and a snail's shell. It works not just because of the drawn similarity between the shell and an igloo – Ham's skill is recognizing the similarity and realizing that it has the potential to make a good cartoon.

This visual pun works through:

a) *The impossible concept of a snail having an igloo.*
b) *The combination of the reaction of the Eskimo and the snail's apparent complacency.*
c) *The fact that snails don't live in the Arctic, hence the surprised expression on the Eskimo's face.*

Cartoonist's tip

If you do need some words to make a joke work use them. Silent jokes can still use annotation, labels and signposts if it helps, as you can see from Pilbrow's cartoon on page 19.

Ham Khan

Warning

Unless you have a specific visual pun or something that lends itself to a captionless joke, don't try and force it; it won't work.

The impossible

A large part of humour and cartoons relies on surprise. As a cartoonist is not restricted to physical laws in his or her drawings they have free rein to let the imagination run riot. This works particularly well with silent cartoons as these can take on the slapstick element of old silent movies. If you don't have words you have to surprise your audience with things they could not see in the real world.

In the image below Angonoa has created humour by depicting the impossible, with the victim continuing to react at what is happening to him. Physical comedy like this does not need words. This cartoon works for two main reasons: first, there is the surprise that someone's tooth is stronger than their neck; and second, it plays on our fear of dentists.

Cartoonist's tip

The advantage of silent cartoons is that they do not need translation and can be sold easily to markets that do not speak your language. Angonoa, for example, lives in Argentina but his cartoon would be equally funny in Britain or Japan. In this case the drawing acts as a communal language, showing a humorous situation that could be universally applied.

▼ *Notice in Angonoa's cartoon how he accentuates the action with just a few movement lines. Here the action is the actual joke so the movement has to look obvious to the viewer.*

Angonoa

Angonoa

Cartoon workout

My example here harks back to silent movies. Once I had conceived of the idea that road works might have been invented at about the same time as the wheel I could have written a caption with a caveman saying something about road works. However, my final solution was neater, and the one-upmanship adds to the joke.

▲ This idea started as two competing cavemen creating wheels. Conflict might create humour, but it was hard to depict the concept for the viewer.

▲ I could suggest conflict by creating something that would upset the first inventor. My first thought was a speed limit, then I plumped for road works.

Now it's your turn!

1 Visual puns – practise drawing simple shapes and then turn them into different objects. Once you have a collection of different objects see which ones look like each other. Can you turn them into cartoons?

2 The impossible – imagine the laws of physics do not apply. What would happen if a cleaning lady tried to unblock her vacuum cleaner while it was on?

3 Imagine different road signs that could work for my cartoon example. Can you find one that works better? What about a no parking sign?

◀ This cartoon can only work because the sign is understood to mean road works. Without widespread recognition I would have needed either speech or a caption.

SILLY HUMOUR

Just thinking of someone doing something stupid can be one of the most effective ways of coming up with joke ideas. We all do stupid things and we naturally laugh at both our own silliness and that of others. Stupidity isn't just a matter of getting something wrong; it is about doing something ridiculous. The more strait-laced or frightening the person doing something silly or stupid, the funnier the joke. A person slipping on a banana skin is quite funny, but a dignified person in all their finery slipping on a banana skin is extra funny. You can use this very effectively in cartoons if you can get the right person and the right scenario. Tragedy is a great person falling from a great height, but so is comedy, just done in a different way.

Look at Clive Goddard's cartoon at the bottom of page 29. Depicting the personification of death as a tourist eating ice cream is ridiculous since this is not how we imagine the grim reaper behaving. Even without the punning caption this picture would raise a smile.

Warning

Don't be cruel. Making fun of people only works if the viewer is on your side. An intelligent person being stupid is funny, but an unintelligent person being stupid is not.

Mike Baldwin

Another victim of disorganized crime

CASE STUDY

Look at the cartoon by Mike Baldwin. The concept of disorganized crime is funny in itself. Mike could have poked fun directly at the Mafia, but the joke seems to work better with a mugger being stupid.

Here the humour works because:

a) *Mugging is a frightening notion, so an incompetent mugger breaks the tension and dispels our fears.*

b) *The gun facing the wrong way is just so stupid. No one is that dense. Taking stupidity to its absolute limit allows Mike to make his point visually. A mugger just fumbling a bit would not be so easy to depict or look so ridiculous to the viewer.*

'We feel that you don't appreciate the importance of what we do here.'

Adults as children

Another strain of 'silly cartoons' is adults acting like children. The category still follows the same principles just mentioned, but this time a cartoonist is poking fun at adult seriousness in general rather than at specific 'bogeymen'. The humour comes from both the unexpected and from our need to laugh at our own seriousness.

A good example of this is the cartoon above by Peter King (PaK). We expect nuclear physicists to be serious, we do not expect them to be playing, but the idea that they might be silly is funny. Obviously some of the humour in this comes from a scientist making jewellery from a molecular model, but the real joy of this cartoon is the fact that the characters are drawn like naughty schoolchildren having fun. The molecule in the nose of the childish scientist is the icing on the cake. Imagine a similar joke set in a school chemistry lab. It might work, but there would not be as large a gap between the seriousness of the situation and the silliness of the behaviour.

The Groan Factor

As with all cartoons be careful. Just being stupid is not enough for a good joke. Adults playing on swings is not silly enough to be funny, but businessmen playing on a bouncy castle in their office might be.

▼ *Note how Clive Goddard has used the visual shorthand of a gondola to immediately identify Venice to the viewer.*

Clive Goddard

Death in Venice

Cartoon workout

Silliness and puns go hand in hand. A word that has two meanings can produce some ridiculous imagery. What makes the cartoon here silly, though, is the idea of a business catch phrase turning into a real location and the playfulness of the balls.

Now it's your turn!

▲ I had the pun 'whole different ball park', but what would a 'different ball park' look like? A stadium seemed the obvious choice, but this wasn't very visually interesting.

▲ I liked the idea of different types of balls used in my initial doodle. So I expanded on this idea and decided to draw different shaped balls that looked silly and therefore funny.

1 Look at the following scary or authoritative figures and imagine them doing something stupid or ridiculous. Try and make their stupidity relevant to their character.

- **Company chairman**
- **Hitler**
- **The US President**

2 Now Imagine Hitler on the French coast preparing for the invasion of Britain with his generals. If they acted like incompetent children how would they behave? Draw up your idea and then compare it to the one on page 41.

3 Look again at the cartoon on page 16. Redraw it in your own style, but this time have God found in an even more unusual location.

'This is a whole different ball park.'

◄ I like the idea of friendly balls, but I could change the feel of the cartoon by making them look menacing.

EXAGGERATION

In order for the viewer to understand the point or comment you are making the easiest method is to exaggerate what you want to imply as much as possible. Take your idea and then see how far you can stretch it without losing the point.

Humour, as we have just seen, is often about the ridiculous. The more you exaggerate an idea the sillier it becomes and therefore the more funny. A small, but useful, example of this would be a cartoon with a sales graph. Showing the graph dipping slightly would not be visually easy to convey or funny. Showing the graph crashing off the chart, through the floor and heading towards Australia might be.

Adey Bryant

CASE STUDY

This cartoon by Adey Bryant illustrates the point perfectly. The joke Adey is making is about having a flight simulator for passengers as opposed to pilots. Within this idea he is clearly making an observation about how little space there is for passengers in economy class. If he did this realistically it would just be a picture of people sitting in seats.

The humour here is created by:

a) *Conveying to the viewer just how uncomfortable economy class is, by showing the passengers with their knees round their ears.*
b) *The expressions of the passengers, which adds to the effect. These do not have to be exaggerated, however, as their looks of stoicism (as if they were on a real flight) work better than anything more extreme.*

Different forms of exaggeration

Exaggeration in cartoons is not just a way of magnifying a point. Sometimes it can be the point of the joke itself. Look at the picture here by Alan de la Nougerede. In this cartoon Alan is looking for a way of showing the arrogance of the man. The more magnificent the scene the more ridiculous the man's statement becomes. Note that Alan has exaggerated both the beauty of the landscape and the 'averageness' of the man himself, thereby increasing even further the gap between them. The only clue we have as to the source of the man's hubris is the Rolls Royce parked next to the couple. This visual clue tells us that the man's wealth is the source of his arrogance. His companion's lack of expression aids the humour; an overly dramatic reaction would draw the reader's eye away from the landscape, which is the main point of the joke.

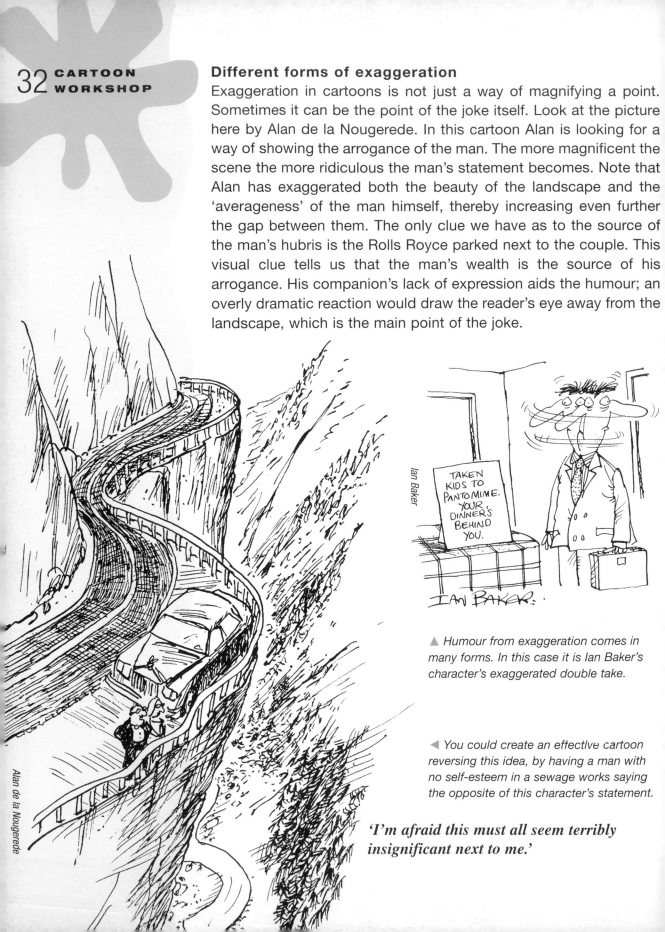

Ian Baker

TAKEN KIDS TO PANTOMIME. YOUR DINNER'S BEHIND YOU.

IAN BAKER

▲ Humour from exaggeration comes in many forms. In this case it is Ian Baker's character's exaggerated double take.

◄ You could create an effective cartoon reversing this idea, by having a man with no self-esteem in a sewage works saying the opposite of this character's statement.

Alan de la Nougerede

'I'm afraid this must all seem terribly insignificant next to me.'

Cartoon workout

Exaggeration does not just have to be physical; it can be conceptual as well. In this cartoon I've used exaggeration to highlight the media notion of dumbing down. By stretching the concept to include the 'dumbest' group that I could think of – clowns – I can make a point about how far I think dumbing down might go, and express people's concerns.

▲ My original idea was to have a clown reading the news, but the viewer wouldn't understand it was a dumbing-down reference.

I worry that the news is dumbing down

▲ My second attempt seemed to put the point across, but it was rather obvious and laboured. So I went for the option below.

Now it's your turn!

1 Look at the cartoon by Mike Stokoe on page 17. Redraw it in your own style but exaggerating the experiment even further. How far can you stretch before the joke gets lost?

2 Draw a cartoon based on the phrase 'Yep, that was one serious paper cut.'

3 Look at the cartoon on page 95 in Cartoon Showcase. How do your pictures compare? Note how this cartoon is both silly and exaggerated.

'They want us to dumb down.'

◄ If this scene was drawn with newsreaders rather than clowns it would not be funny, just a statement of fact.

SATIRE

Satire has a specific meaning. It is not really a technique for humour, but rather a subject area. Collins English Dictionary defines it as a medium by which 'topical issues, folly or evil are held up to scorn by means of ridicule and irony'. However, in reality for the cartoonist it means ridiculing serious issues or areas of public life which he or she regards as stupid, silly or worthy of comment. A cartoon about the destruction of the rain forest would be satire. A joke about penguins looking a bit like they wear tuxedos would not – unless, of course, penguins attained high public office.

'Be careful. As soon as you set out to do 'satire' you can get into trouble. In calling yourself a 'satirist' you are in danger of taking yourself too seriously to be funny.'

Giles Pilbrow

Cartoonist's tip

Note in Deacon's cartoon how a cartoonist can set a scene with a single word. By using the name 'Fidel' the viewer automatically thinks that he is somewhere in South or Central America. If Deacon had used the name 'Hank' we may have suspected CIA involvement.

CASE STUDY

Dave Connaughton's (Deacon's) cartoon below is classic satire. The artist's skill is selecting a subject area worthy of comment. If anyone deserves to be attacked by ridicule it is a dictator.

Here the humour is produced by:

a) Our enjoyment at making scary or powerful figures look silly. Deacon achieves this not by the joke, which is a serious issue, but by the way he has drawn his character. We immediately recognize the man as a 'jumped-up' leader with his medals, braid and sunglasses that are all worn to intimidate.

b) The fact that we naturally imagine that this is how such a leader would conduct his elections, and laugh with recognition when we see the stereotype depicted.

Dave Connaughton (Deacon)

'Fidel – Do you have next month's election results?'

Clive Goddard

'What is public transport exactly?'

A rich area for ideas

Satire, like observational humour, is about selecting subjects that people will identify with and that act as springboards for humour. If something makes you angry or you see stupidity, cruelty or injustice someone else will share that feeling. Finding humour in your target requires some of the techniques we have already discussed, such as exaggeration, puns and being silly, but it also requires precise skills of its own. If you get it right the viewer will laugh because you have struck a nerve.

In Clive Goddard's cartoon above, about public transport policy, Clive manages a swipe at both our out of touch politicians and the transport policy itself. Public transport policy is controlled by politicians who we assume do not use public transport themselves. By observing and highlighting this irony, and exaggerating the politician's ignorance, Clive manages to satirize both the policy makers and the policy.

▼ *Richard Jolley's cartoon comments on the rise in underage pregnancy by exaggerating the extra demand for maternity wear by schoolgirls.*

Richard Jolley

Cartoon workout

Everyone enjoys hating the press, so they are a good topic for ridicule. Exaggeration always works well for satire so in this cartoon I wanted to illustrate the commonly held notion that journalists are the lowest form of life. I took the phrase literally and put them just behind the amoebae in the evolutionary line.

© Private Eye

▲ I had recently drawn another cartoon using an evolutionary progression, and it was this cartoon that was in my mind when I was thinking about how to show how low the press had sunk recently.

▲ Cartoonists have a pictorial shorthand for certain professions. I knew it wouldn't be difficult to convey the concept of a journalist to the viewer. I drew a quick sketch of the character I wanted.

1 Write down a list of figures or professions that you think are worthy of lampooning. Redraw my cartoon in your own style but place a different figure at the back of the evolutionary line. Politicians, lawyers and accountants all work as well.

2 Try and remember some corporate/ political slogans or names of organizations that you can twist. Here are a couple to get you started:

- **Military Intelligence**
- **The bank that likes to say yes**

▼ Then it was just a matter of putting the two pictures together. To make my point more strongly I deliberately put the journalist behind the lowest form of life I could think of – an amoeba.

ANTHROPOMORPHISM

What do Garfield, Snoopy and Scooby Doo have in common? They are all animals behaving like humans, which is what the word anthropomorphism means for cartoonists. The animals retain some of their species attributes – for instance, Garfield, the famous cartoon cat, hates dogs, but as a general rule cats don't philosophize on life, eat lasagne or hate Mondays.

Animals acting human

Imagining how animals would behave if they were more like human beings is rich territory for creating cartoons. Anthropomorphism allows the cartoonist to use both animal behaviour to make comments about ourselves and human behaviour to derive humour from animals. Using animals is often a useful visual metaphor. If you need an idea for a cartoon about drinking at work imagining a scenario with a St Bernard dog wearing a brandy-barrel collar isn't a bad start.

Cartoonist's tip

Animals work in a cartoon only if the viewer understands the parallels that are being made. A joke about an obscure animal is unlikely to work.

Ron Therien

Fluffy's first and last day as an exchange student

CASE STUDY

In this cartoon Canadian Ron Therien has created humour by imagining animals in a human world. Ron knows that any audience will understand the traditional enmity between cats and dogs and it works as a visual shorthand for humans not getting along. He has used that to imagine the worst possible school-exchange scenario.

The comic effect relies on:

a) The shared realization of how badly exchange visits can go wrong.
b) Our natural amusement at how much cats and dogs dislike each other.
c) The use of exaggeration to imagine the worst scenario.
d) The fact that we find the idea of animals in a human context appealing.

Highlighting observations of ourselves

Drawing parallels between human and animal behaviour is a useful way of highlighting observations of ourselves. The viewer laughs (it is hoped) for all the usual reasons (surprise, recognition, etc.), but the effect is heightened because we like to think of ourselves as a higher form of life. Pointing out our similarities to animals bursts the bubble of our own pomposity or those we are commenting on.

In the cartoon below by Isabella Bannerman parallels are taken to an extreme. Here we do not have an animal displaying human behaviour, but a human exhibiting his animal side. In this case the target is untidy men. We believe that we have evolved beyond marking our own territory as a dog would, but showing man's animal side and comparing it to a dog makes a good and funny point. However, it is very different from a cartoon where the animals are acting like humans, as illustrated on page 37.

> 'You've already grabbed your audience if you've got an animal talking. There is something about them that makes even a mundane statement coming from a speaking dog funny.'

Duncan McCoshan
(Knife)

Cartoonist's tip

Note in Isabella's cartoon that though the illustration is stylized she has not tried to draw 'funny'. The humour comes through because the more subtle drawing style allows the viewer to see the untidiness and the dog as realistic and the parallels become more believable.

Isabella Bannerman

How animals mark their territory

Cartoon workout

We have all seen the 'and finally' section of the news where a parrot who can skateboard is used as light relief after reports of wars and politics. Here I have used the 'what if' technique in conjunction with anthropomorphism to imagine an animal newscaster ending a bulletin.

▲ This cartoon started as a doodle of a dog sitting up at a table. I put a piece of paper in front of him and he reminded me of a newsreader.

▲ Once I had my dog newsreader, I imagined what dog news would be like and what their 'and finally' item might be. The final version was then easy.

'… and finally …'

Now it's your turn!

1 Look at the list of three animals below. Write down what human characteristics best define them (for example, cats are arrogant, dogs are loyal).

- **Goldfish**
- **Weasel**
- **Lion**

2 Now think of human situations where these characteristics would be seen. For example, if dogs are loyal it might be funny to depict one as a customer at an unhelpful bank.

3 Imagine dogs watching a home video. What would it be? Draw up a cartoon and then compare it to the one on page 52. Were you thinking on the same lines?

◀ The saying 'less is more' applies to this caption. The viewer can understand the scenario in just two words.

Subject matter

Now you've mastered the basic techniques for constructing jokes you'll need subjects to tell jokes about. This is half the battle. Obviously any subject can be a subject for humour, but there are certain categories that provide the perfect springboard for creating good cartoons.

HISTORY

One of the best springboards for humour is events and peoples from history. History cartoons can be a simple joke about the past. The distance of time means we are less close to the emotions of the period and can be silly about serious subjects. A joke about the *Titanic* could be funny. A joke about a recent disaster would not be. However, history jokes work best where they are saying something about the modern world. Historic events and figures can work as a shorthand to explain and comment on events in the present.

CASE STUDY

Using anachronism is an effective way of finding humour in the past and making fun of the present. An anachronism for a cartoonist is where something or someone is out of their natural historical context. A zebra crossing placed at Moses' parting of the Red Sea would be a good example. In this cartoon Mike Baldwin has imagined a caveman computer dating.

What makes this cartoon funny is:

a) The anachronism of a caveman using a stone computer. This sight raises a smile in itself because it is ridiculous.

b) Mike's great choice of dating as the subject. The concept of a caveman looking for a date raises the question of what he would look for in a partner. Mike's conceit is that even with a computer a caveman's interests would be pretty limited.

Mike Baldwin

'Rugged romantic seeks elegant lady. Must like hunting and gathering.'

Using historical moments

Using a historical context allows the cartoonist to add more depth to a joke. Modern frustrations, such as not having the right change, are sometimes hard to convey to the viewer in a fresh and original way.

Mike Williams has achieved a successful cartoon by using Hitler and his cronies as a platform for an aspect of life that nearly everyone can relate to. The cartoon is funny because he has chosen a major historical event and has brought it down to a human level. The viewer

Mike Williams

'Gott in Himmel! Somebody must have a franc!!!'

is instantly aware that Hitler standing on cliffs looking out to sea is a symbol for the possible invasion of Britain. Since this concept is part of a shared psyche Mike can therefore use it as a symbol for danger we will understand. Once he has this threatening symbol he can relieve our anxiety by making the people do something childish or silly and therefore make us laugh. If he had used tourists looking out across the channel, we wouldn't have been able to identify it as the English Channel and their lack of change would not be funny.

Warning

You can only use history if the reader is likely to know about the event. Few people will pick up a reference to 18th-century land reform, for instance.

Cartoon workout

In the cartoon below I wanted to poke fun at the modern phenomenon of the sound bite. I realized that by selecting a famous historic speech I could highlight the change in society and make the phenomenon look silly.

▲ I needed a historic speech and character that people would recognize instantly, and would respect enough to make a sound-bite version seem silly.

▲ My first thought was a crowd scene, but at this scale it would be hard to recognize Lincoln or tell that he was giving the Gettysburg Address.

1 Look at the following historical characters and aspects of modern life. Which go best together?

- **Noah**
- **Channel tunnel**
- **Marriage counselling**
- **Napoleon**
- **Weather forecasters**
- **Henry VIII**

2 Create a cartoon based around the best combination of character and modern phenomenon. I like the idea of Henry VIII as a marriage counsellor.

3 How would Gengis Khan react to a customs official? Select your own event from the past and find a modern parallel. If you can't do it this way round select a modern frustration and find a historic event that can symbolize it.

'Now can we have it as a sound bite?'

◄ Note how I haven't had to draw an accurate caricature of Lincoln. The beard is enough for the viewer to recognize him.

CURRENT AFFAIRS

Current affairs are a staple for a lot of cartoonists. Magazines such as *Private Eye* always need fresh material about the events of the day. Changing events provide ample opportunity for cartoonists to exercise their wit. The important point to remember is to choose your topic carefully. If the major news story is about events in the Middle East, drawing cartoons about a dinner-lady strike in Doncaster is not going to appeal to many editors or readers. You want to be covering the stories that everyone is talking about, not the ones that lend themselves most easily to a quick joke.

CASE STUDY

Look at Clive Goddard's cartoon on the right. If one topic has dominated British politics for the last ten years it is Europe and the euro. Like all good cartoons the success of the cartoon depends on the reader instantly understanding the point that Clive is making. Clive wants the viewer to grasp the point quickly that our culture is already influenced by others so the irony of the euro protesters' message is understood. To do this he shows the influence of American culture by dressing his character in a baseball cap, a New York T-shirt and clutching a can of Coke.

The cartoonist makes his point by:

a) *Giving the man a placard so we see what he represents.*
b) *Picking symbols that can be depicted and understood quickly (such as Nike and Coke).*
c) *Using little background detail, so the focus is on the protester's clothes.*

Clive Goddard

Richard Jolley

'Hi! It's me. I'm on a gravy train …'

▼ *Combine a swipe at politicians with another news story and you will hit the mark, as Robert Thompson demonstrates.*

Robert Thompson

'Human cloning, what a terrifying thought.'

Perennial topics

There are really two types of current affairs cartoon. The first are major news stories, but news changes so fast that you need to work quickly with these or you will miss the moment. The second type of stories are ones that are always in the news and run for years. Topics that never seem to date include anything to do with the EU and euro, global warming and the environment, British trains, the Middle East and genetic science. Clive Goddard's cartoon on page 43 or Richard Jolley's cartoon above, though related to current affairs, were as relevant five years ago as they are now. We continue to find humour in them as long as they concern an issue that people can get angry about or have an opinion about, so enjoy seeing them lampooned. However, once they stop being newsworthy the viewer will quickly stop finding them funny because they will not care about the topic any more.

Cartoon workout

Politicians are always blaming others for their mistakes. The cartoon below was originally drawn to illustrate an article for a civil servant publication, but it could apply equally to any situation where politicians are passing the buck.

 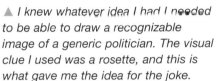 

▲ I knew whatever idea I had I needed to be able to draw a recognizable image of a generic politician. The visual clue I used was a rosette, and this is what gave me the idea for the joke.

▲ In my first attempt I gave the politician glasses and a cheesy grin, but on reflection he looked too much like a doctor with glasses, and the grin was too harsh for the point the article was making.

1 Look at this list of topics. Which do you think will be on-going stories and which will not occur again for a while?

- **Destruction of the rainforest**
- **Human cloning**
- **Striking miners**

2 Cloning is often in the news at the moment, as can be seen in the cartoon opposite. Think of an idea for a cloning joke set in a maternity ward and compare it to the one on page 57.

3 Watch the news this evening and see if you can guess which stories cartoonists will choose for tomorrow's newspapers.

◄ The rosette had to be larger than normal so that the viewer can read the words, but it also adds to the humour.

RELATIONSHIPS

Friction between people, especially couples, is always a fine area for humour. Where there is discord there is usually room for humour, and as everyone has been in one sort of relationship or another the opportunities to strike a chord with the viewer are endless. The beauty of this topic is that whatever your sex your observations will be understood and appreciated by at least half the population.

Women's perspective on men
There is obviously going to be a difference between how the sexes view their opponents in the sex war and cartoonists find this a rich vein to mine. Though there are no set rules, female cartoonists tend to concentrate on highlighting direct observations in which the joke is an exaggeration of their own or men's behaviour. They find humour in the psychological differences between the sexes. Unsurprisingly, men prefer to see themselves in more simple terms.

Isabella Bannerman

CASE STUDY

Isabella Bannerman's cartoon is definitely from a female perspective. She is sharing a female frustration with her audience, but in a sympathetic way that does not prevent men enjoying the joke. In any relationship joke the skill is to find a point of reference that everyone understands. Note that Isabella has not had to exaggerate, or ridicule anything to get a laugh.

Isabella's skill lies in:

a) *Highlighting a situation to which everyone can relate.*
b) *Packaging the observation as a satire on self help.*
c) *Showing sympathy for both men and women in a common situation.*

Mark Milligan (Markie)

▼ More old-fashioned jokes can still work even if we can't relate to them directly. We still recognize the style of character used.

'Leave those … Kevin'll do the washing up.'

Men's perspective on women

Male cartoonists tend to take a different approach, generally going for a straight gag that uses exaggeration to highlight their observations. In the cartoon above by Robert Thompson, Robert has taken the idea of the hen-pecked husband to the nth degree. He has imagined the most extreme situation he can within marriage to make his point. Robert's approach is less sympathetic than Isabella's, but it will still work with both men and women, because a woman will recognize the bride as a type of woman, rather than representing all women.

Any perspective

You do not have to have an axe to grind to create a successful relationship cartoon, just a knowledge of the subject. As soon as you pick relationships as a topic you have won half the battle because whatever aspect you choose someone is going to smile with recognition (unless, of course, they are a hermit).

'… And it's no use you pleading with me to stay!'

Cartoon workout

Sometimes just a straight depiction of the differences between the sexes can work. In my cartoon below all I wanted to say was that men seem to think about sex more than women – only a little exaggeration was required.

Now it's your turn!

▲ In my initial sketch I was drawing a literal interpretation of my first thought. The magazines my figures held made me think of the difference between women's and men's magazines.

▲ This version was a bit too subtle, and as the joke was now as much about magazines as about men and women, I decided to widen the focus and plumped for the version below.

1 Look below at the list of sweeping relationship generalizations. Which ones do you think would require exaggeration and which ones a more subtle approach in a cartoon?

- **Men never hoover without being asked**
- **Women don't like football**
- **Boyfriends never ring when they are supposed to**

2 Redraw my cartoon *(left)* in your own style and replace the magazine titles with ones of your own. Can you create a different joke using the same concept?

3 Redraw the cartoons on pages 40 and 47, but try swapping the gender roles. Which ones work both ways round?

◄ The final version could have worked equally well if I had used sport or cars instead of sex under the 'men's interest' category.

PROFESSIONS AND WORK

A huge part of our lives is consumed with work. We all have to do it, we all talk about it and we all have our favourite hated professions. We appear to have a collective consciousness of the character traits of certain professions such as lawyers and accountants even if we have no direct contact with those groups ourselves. While other stereotypes (such as racial and sexual) have, quite rightly, become frowned upon it is our good fortune that we can still legitimately attack people for the work they do.

Shorthand and symbols

Cartooning is a medium that relies greatly on symbols to convey a concept immediately. Some professions, notably lawyers and accountants, are instantly associated with characteristics such as greed, deviousness, dullness, etc. that are prime targets for comedy. The humour works not only because we are aware of the symbols but because everyone is happy to laugh at a group that is considered to be powerful.

Cartoonist's tip

Drawing a cartoon about something conceptual, such as being boring, is hard because it's difficult to illustrate 'boring' – accountants, on the other hand, are easy to draw.

Jerry King

'See, I told you sharks don't attack lawyers.
It's a respect thing.'

CASE STUDY

Jerry King's cartoon shows how a profession can be shorthand for certain characteristics. He is comparing the stereotype of a lawyer – that is, greedy unprincipled and avaricious – to a shark. His skill lies in not saying 'lawyers are all a bunch of sharks' – that would be a cliché.

Jerry's cartoon works through:

a) *Surprise – we have to read the caption and then look back at the picture before we can see what's happening.*
b) *Literally imagining sharks can act like human beings.*
c) *Making the lawyer look as nerdy as possible so the shark's respect is highlighted.*

Pete Dredge

'...THE FIRST HOUR IS FREE SO LET'S SIT BACK AND ENJOY THESE PANORAMIC VIEWS OF THE ANDES'

Warning

Obviously not all professions are interchangeable. Not many people would find Pete Dredge's joke *(right)* funny if the scenario was in a travel agents or even a projector salesman's office. If you have a point to make be sure to choose the right occupation.

▼ *In Duncan McCoshan's (Knife's) cartoon look how the clown is a shorthand for one extreme and accountants for another.*

Interchangeability

If you look again at Jerry King's cartoon on page 49 and substituted the words 'tabloid journalist' for the word lawyer the joke would still be funny. This is because the joke was not about lawyers, but about a certain set of attributes. This is a boon for a cartoonist as the same sort of jokes can be used for many different purposes. Look at the Pete Dredge cartoon above. The desk sign reads 'senior consultant', but Pete could sell the same cartoon to Lawyer Weekly, Doctor Monthly or Taxi Driver Digest by using just a small amount of correction fluid.

Please note that although I have concentrated on professionals in this section any job will have traits that will work as shorthand for cartoons. Even caring professions such as nursing will be useful to you if you need to symbolize a characteristic that is positive.

Duncan McCoshan (Knife)

'I'm going to run away and join a firm of accountants.'

Cartoon workout

It's not only professionals who are worthy of comment. In my cartoon below I was trying to air my frustrations at bank clerks, but again the same idea would work for any job where advice is given with a condescending attitude. When I drew the expression I knew I wouldn't need a punch line. It would be instantly recognizable.

▲ Some cartoons seem to flow out of the pen. I needed to add very little once I had drawn this simple character sketch.

▲ My only skill was recognizing the face as interesting and finding a context for it, by expressing my prejudices and experiences.

Now it's your turn!

1 Look at these character traits and jobs. Match the right traits to the right jobs:
- taxi driver
- undertaker
- scientist
- absent-minded
- un-politically correct
- gloomy

2 If you wanted to make a point about vanity you might choose to attack a rock star. Look at these concepts and decide on the profession that best embodies each one:
- job's-worth
- overcharging
- meanness

3 Look again at Jerry King's cartoon on page 49. Redraw it in your own style, but find a new profession that sharks would respect. Does the cartoon work?

◀ In the final drawing I shaded the jacket and the sign to focus the viewer's eye on the character's face.

ANIMALS

Animals make great subject matter even when cartoonists are not insisting on giving them human traits or comparing our own behaviour to theirs. Animals are funny just when they act like animals. We all giggle at home-video TV shows of puppies chasing their tails and kittens attacking small balls of string. Cartoonists can utilize this natural inclination to their own advantage. Remember, though, that this is not anthropomorphism. This is about how animals actually act and how we interact with them.

CASE STUDY

Look at the cartoon on the right by Oliver Preston. Oliver creates a warm family scene of pet owners with their dogs. With the exception of the smiles on the dogs' faces to indicate pleasure this is definitely dogs acting like dogs. Oliver is not making the dogs talk or stand on two legs to reflect human behaviour. The dogs are just being 'doggy'. As with all cartoons, though, Oliver's skill does not come from just noting that dogs don't like cats.

The humour works through:

a) *Using contrasting expressions on the human and dogs' faces to highlight the gulf between how we and dogs see the world.*

b) *The figure composition, which allows the artist to show that though pet owners think they are in charge their pets dominate. The viewer gets the feeling that the people would like to watch something else, but they don't want to upset their pets.*

Oliver Preston

'Isn't this the video of how the cat got run over?'

Claudic Furnier

The bizarre animal world

Humour with animals does not just come from our pets and the 'funny things they do'. The whole animal kingdom is populated by a cast of bizarre and unusual creatures that are ripe for exploration. An elephant looks 'funny' even before the cartoonists get to work. With his big ears and trunk a cartoonist is pretty much pushing at an open door to find a way of using an elephant for humour. In the cartoon above Claudio Furnier has used the unusual build of a pelican to create a visual joke. In exaggerating what a pelican can hold in his bill Furnier highlights just how unusual pelicans are. To prove this joke is about pelicans imagine if the diver was caught by a trawlerman – less funny, huh?

Werner Wejp-Olsen

'Well, Bella – convinced?'

Cartoon workout

In my slightly poor-taste animal joke you don't even get to see the animal. My initial idea was a joke about animals and vets. As soon as I thought of vets, I latched onto the TV series *Animal Hospital* ...

▲ *Rolf Harris is a gift for cartoonists. Once I focused on* Animal Hospital, *finding something funny Rolf could do was just a matter of writing down his 'trademarks' until inspiration struck.*

▲ *Caricature is a separate discipline from gag cartoons. I didn't have time to get the likeness right, but other visual indicators, like the hospital sign, beard and glasses would be enough.*

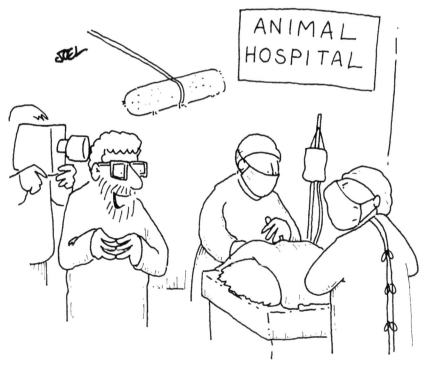

'Can you tell what it is yet?'

Now it's your turn!

1 Cats are great subject matter. Look at this list of traits and select the ones that best describe a cat:

- **lazy**
- **faithful**
- **independent**
- **selfish**
- **loving**

2 Now imagine a scenario of cats sharing a bed with their owners and draw it up. Then compare it to the cartoon on page 95 in the Gallery section.

3 Look again at Claudio Furnier's pelican cartoon on page 53. Using a similar idea, imagine the best scenario you can where pelicans are competing against trawler fishermen and draw it up into a finished cartoon.

◀ *In the finished version I used a quick sketch of a sound boom as visual shorthand for a professional TV recording.*

SCICENCE

If there's one area that can kick-start the imagination it is science. In science anything is possible; it allows creators to imagine the impossible within a plausible context. The areas that can be covered within science are endless: mad scientists, new technology, animal experimentation, science's real and imagined impact – and the great thing is you don't even need the maths.

Fantasy science

As science fiction in literature allows comment about the present by looking to the future, science in cartoons allows cartoonists to make comments and jokes using the same formula. For example, time machines don't exist but they are useful devices around which to create humour. So if you want to do a great joke about commuting why not have people flying to work and set it in the future?

Keith Clayton

'Why, no! I thought you said you made the antidote.'

CASE STUDY

Keith Clayton has used fantasy science to create the gag for his cartoon. The basic joke here is about people's forgetfulness and incompetence. Forgetfulness could be funny in itself, but it really needs an amusing consequence to work successfully. By using 'mad scientists' Keith can exaggerate the potential dilemma created by forgetfulness.

The situation is made funny by:

a) *Using scientists to create a believable scenario for the extreme exaggeration.*
b) *Our expectation that scientists are competent. Depicting them as foolish is unexpected and funny.*
c) *Keith shrinking the scientists instead of turning them into monsters. This increases the dilemma facing them and we can imagine these small people trying to fix the problem.*

Don't just pick a specific scientific change, since it may date quickly. Science's methods, however, can give you an ample platform. Look at the two cartoons on this page to see what I mean.

▼ *Cartoons can always fit into more than one category. Kevin Smith's (Kes's) joke is about animal experimentation, but it is also a cartoon built on anthropomorphism.*

Andy McKay (Naf)

'*... I can therefore conclude that the primates are indeed social animals.*'

Kevin Smith (Kes)

'*No thanks, I've started rolling my own.*'

Real science

Science is not just a tool for believable fantasy. The formal process of experimentation that is used in scientific work can be the source of much humour. Real science and its impact on our world can also be fruitful for the cartoonist. Most people have a reaction to change (both positive and negative) and science is the engine of so much change. Change is great for jokes as it allows the cartoonist to compare how things are to how things might be and point out the potential ridiculousness.

Look at my cartoon *(right)*. Cloning may or may not prove to be a good or a bad thing, but by making a comparison between how things are now and how things might be in the future I have (I hope) struck a chord and made a comment that people will relate to.

Cartoon workout

Science cartoons don't have to have scientists in them. I wanted to make a joke about cloning, but I also wanted to highlight how this area of science would affect all of us. Scientists in the cartoon would have made the joke more about their characters than about the effects their discoveries and work might have on society.

▲ When I started I thought that people looking the same was comic in itself, but I had seen similar ideas before.

▲ I preferred this second version, but the punch line needed work and I thought the obvious clone of the mother unnecessary.

'Ooh she's got your eyes, and nose, mouth ...'

Now it's your turn!

1 Look again at the cartoon by Keith Clayton on page 55. Using the same punch line draw your own cartoon. Stretch your imagination as much as possible to imagine a scenario that would be equally funny. Would it work if the scientists had been turned into frogs?

2 There would be little point cloning things if they already looked identical to each other. Using this notion, create a cartoon about cloning sheep.

◄ I finally found a better punch line that got over the point I was making in a more subtle and fresher way.

I assume that after the expert tuition in the first section you are now brimming over with workable cartoon ideas and have the know-how to create even more. However, the ideas on their own are only half the battle. Remember a cartoon is a combination of an idea and how the artist gets that idea across to the audience. You may have thought of the funniest joke on the planet but you still have the task of making sure that the audience will quickly understand the point you want to make.

This book is not about how to draw cartoons but even if your drawing skills are quite limited this next

VING

section will explain how different drawing styles appeal to different audiences and how varying your style can heighten the humour in your work. A lot of the humour in a cartoon can come from the drawing itself, and it's as true to say that a good idea can be lost by a poor drawing as it is that an average idea can be improved by a well-illustrated one. I will show you how to target your audience and identify the different styles of cartoon that appeal to these markets. I'll also cover how to use expression, focus, movement, shading, scale and captioning to get the most out of the ideas you create and offer advice for when things go wrong!

Right drawing right joke

Go into a newsagent's and look at the vast number of different publications that cater to different audiences and tastes. Youth, satire, political, hobby, lifestyle magazines, tabloid and broadsheet newspapers all require a slightly different approach.

TARGET YOUR AUDIENCE

💣☀️**Warning**

Sending the wrong style of joke or drawing to a publication will irritate editors as it will indicate that you have not read their publication before submitting. Irritating an editor is never a good idea.

▶ *This cartoon and the one opposite both satirize the rise of New Labour. In this cartoon I tried to add extra humour by making the figures 'funny', with the short attention span of puppies.*

Though the general public tends to see cartoonists as a homogenous group and one cartoon as much the same as another, editors and design editors are generally looking for a specific feel for their publication. A political publication, which has an educated readership, requires not only a sophisticated joke, but a drawing style to match. A mass-circulation tabloid or a puzzle magazine is more likely to be looking for 'end of the pier' humour both in the joke and the obvious 'cartoony' approach to the artwork.

Joel Mishon © Private Eye

'We're going to leave the rich alone and just spend the money we have more wisely!'

Joel Mishon © Private Eye

'We're going to leave the rich alone and just spend the money we have more wisely!'

Know your audience

If you are submitting work to a publication look first to see what sort of work it accepts. In the drawings on these two pages I have drawn the same joke in different ways. The version on the left was drawn for and published in the satirical magazine *Private Eye*. The cartoons this publication takes on are, on the whole, simple line drawings used to break up text with a political or social satire subject matter. The drawing style is normally 'dry' – that is, the expressions are deadpan, not overexaggerated, more Jack Dee than Benny Hill.

For the image above I have redrawn the same joke, but in a style that would be more acceptable for an editorial page of a newspaper or political magazine. The drawing has to be more visually interesting so it could be used not just to break up text, but as a feature in itself. As the joke is a satire and would appeal to a similar audience as that of *Private Eye* I have kept the expressions and figures deadpan, but have filled out the picture with more detail and shading and extra figures. This more detailed approach allows the reader to dwell longer on the joke and read more into it if they wish.

'The best way to come up with new ideas is to pay attention to your surroundings; people, objects and nature will provide you with everything you'll ever need.'

Andy McKay (Naf)

Cartoonist's tip

If you can't adapt your style to fit different markets, don't worry. Just work on what you are good at. I've produced work for broadsheets, satire, lifestyle, business and computer magazines, greetings cards, websites, books and newspapers, but never tabloids. I don't have the right feel for that market, so I concentrate on other publications.

TABLOID CARTOONS

If you read the *Sun* or the *Mirror* newspapers you will be familiar with tabloids. A tabloid is a newspaper with smaller pages than a broadsheet, with an emphasis on photographs and a concise and often sensational style. I use the term 'tabloid', therefore, to refer to a certain type of humour and the drawing style that accompanies this editorial approach. It is a slightly unfashionable style now, but it still has a very large audience. The humour tends to have a populist and traditional approach – more Bernard Manning than Eddie Izzard – with punch lines that often feature stereotypical characters. The drawing style is normally friendly with rounded shapes and a lot of facial expression, a bit like you find in children's comics.

Mark Milligan (Markie)

'*Beelzebub I presume?*
On earth I was married to your sister!'

CASE STUDY

Mark Milligan's (Markie's) cartoon is a classic example of tabloid humour. The subject matter is classic 'take my wife – please' music-hall stuff. However, even the most fervent *Guardian* reader would respond to it, because it is a surprising take on what is old subject matter. The drawing style is friendly and uncomplicated and the joke is clearly 'labelled' by the unsubtle expression on the speaker's face and the devil's reaction. Tabloid cartoons tend to go for overstatement, rather than subtlety in the drawing, but the joke, even if it is an old theme, still needs a fresh approach to succeed.

Here the humour is produced by:

a) *The choice of wording. Beelzebub is an archaic word and is funny in itself.*
b) *Making the joke implicit, rather than explicit. It uses the surprise technique. If the speaker was just saying 'my wife is the devil's sister' it would not be funny.*
c) *The devil looks ineffectual, which is funny because it's silly. We don't expect Beelzebub to politely shake hands with someone.*

Adey Bryant

Warning

Don't imagine that a tabloid newspaper uses the cartoons it does because it can't do 'better'. More sophisticated wit or drawing is deliberately not used because it does not suit its audience.

◀ Adey Bryant's cartoon works as a tabloid cartoon because of the drawing style, but the joke is more observational than 'end of the pier', so its market could be wider.

Style workout

If you are going to submit work to publications that take tabloid-style cartoons, you will have to develop a style of drawing that reflects that populist humour style. Obviously everyone has their own way of drawing, and no one should tell you exactly how to draw, but here are a few pointers that might help you produce cartoons aimed specifically at the tabloid market.

- Work on friendly faces with a lot of expression.
- Exaggerate features in a friendly way. Try to go for rounded, rather than angular, lines.
- Try not to use too much shading; simple clean lines work best.
- Focus on the main action. You don't need a cast of thousands or architectural detail.

▲ Practise a tabloid style by drawing expressive friendly faces with rounded shapes, simple lines and no shading.

BROADSHEET CARTOONS

I have called this second style 'broadsheet' to contrast it with the tabloid style, but it really refers to a type of drawing and humour that is seen in magazines such as the old *Punch* magazine and the *New Yorker* as well as broadsheet newspapers such as *The Telegraph*. If you are planning to produce work for the sort of audience that reads the broadsheet press then you will have to use a different humour and drawing style from the one used for the tabloids. The humour required often depends on social and political satire, and appeals to a more sophisticated or more highly educated reader. Accordingly, the drawing style is generally more detailed, understated and/or fashionably quirky than used in tabloid cartoons.

OLIVER PRESTON

Oliver Preston

'**Owing to His Lordship's recent acrimonious divorce, the hall is now open at half price.'**

CASE STUDY

Oliver Preston's cartoon contrasts well with the tabloid style of Mark Milligan on page 62 and has a 'retro' feel of old *Punch* and *New Yorker* cartoons of the 1950s. The humour in his work relies not just on the joke but on a social situation, and the artwork itself has an aesthetic appeal that goes beyond just being funny. The artwork stands alone as an interesting feature in itself and is not just a vehicle for a joke. This style is most commonly seen today in newspapers in the editorial cartoons on the editorial pages. The cartoon is not a quick sketch, but a piece of draughtsmanship that makes full use of scale, architectural detail, wash shading and a range of characters.

The humour here relies on:

a) *The contrast between the detailed artwork and the simple joke, which magnifies the humour. If this joke was drawn in Mark Milligan's style it wouldn't have such impact.*

b) *The understated and slightly bemused expressions of the characters, which adds additional contrast to the havoc of the scene.*

John McGillen

'I say we shoot anyone who claims
we broke the ceasefire …'

Cartoonist's tip

The same joke idea can work for two different publications if the drawing style is different. Try redrawing Mark Milligan's cartoon on page 62 so that it might appeal to a 'broadsheet' audience.

◀ *Note how there is nothing 'crowd pleasing' about John McGillen's work. The characters are not drawn to look cute, but to fit with the subject matter of the joke.*

Style workout

Crosshatching and line shading seem to complement the more biting jokes that are associated with broadsheet humour. Shading can add a spikiness and depth that reflects the atmosphere of the joke. In John McGillen's cartoon above the drawing style has an 'ugliness' that complements the subject matter. If you have a 'broadsheet joke' try:

- Creating a more hard-hitting style by using more angular lines in your drawing.
- Underplaying the expression to get a more deadpan feel and make the faces less friendly.
- Using line and crosshatch shading to add 'grit'.
- Adding more detail so the picture is a feature in itself and not just used to break up text.

▲ *I created these figures by looking at my 'tabloid' sketches on page 63 and using more 'broadsheet' techniques.*

QUIRKY CARTOONS

As with all things there are fashions in cartooning. In the section on tabloid style on pages 62–3 I mentioned that the drawing style and jokes tended to be 'traditional'. As a reaction to this approach some publications and cartoonists have tried to break the mould by offering a more quirky off-beat style. The jokes are generally more biting and often surreal and the drawing style more individual. Though the figures might still be considered 'cute', they are generally more deadpan and the shapes used more idiosyncratic.

Quirky cartooning is about adding your own personality and vision. The humour generally comes from having a different way of seeing the world. There are no rules as such other than your own individual statement. The techniques for creating jokes are much as already mentioned for a traditional approach, but there is a tendency towards silly and more observational humour.

Warning

Don't draw in a 'weird' style for the sake of it. Find a style that both reflects your humour and will appeal to the reader.

Peter King (PaK)

'He's away from his desk at the moment, but he'll be back in a second …'

CASE STUDY

Peter King (PaK) has found a very individual style that could easily be described as quirky. He has created a world populated with cute and childish, but ugly, gnome-like people who don't seem to behave according to standard rules. As his world is self-contained he can make his characters behave in a way that would seem stupid, rather than humorous, if drawn in a more traditional style.

Humour here is produced by:

a) *The strange childlike characters, which make the situation strangely believable.*
b) *As the situation is believable we can suspend disbelief and enjoy the surprising pun.*

ALMEIDA

Arnaldo Almeida

'I think Charlie is taking Casual Fridays a bit too far!'

◄ *Arnaldo Almeida uses similar squat figures to Peter King (PaK), but his work has a different feel because of his more friendly expressions and cleaner shading.*

Style workout

Populating your cartoons with unusual, non-traditional cartoon characters will add humour to your work because it will seem fresher, in the same way that an alternative comic can make a traditional joke seem fresh and funny. Body shape is as important as facial features to create a quirky style. Don't just experiment with different figures and faces. Try different pens and shading techniques till you find one that works for you. Arnaldo Almeida *(see above)* uses a computer to colour his work, which has become very much part of his style.

- Practise drawing faces and different head shapes until you find a combination that matches your sense of humour.
- Now do the same with different body shapes until you find one that suits the heads you have created.
- See what other effects aid your humour, such as shading, washes or pen and brush effects.

▲ *Note how, in my sketches, different combinations of noses and eyes create different character designs.*

ILLUSTRATIVE CARTOONS

Often when we think of a cartoon we think of a quick sketch, but a great deal of humour can be added to a simple joke by taking a more illustrative approach. Large well-illustrated cartoons often add to humour by providing a contrast between the beauty or detail of the picture with the silliness of the joke. This contrast makes us laugh for the same reasons that silliness and exaggeration make us laugh. Essentially the viewer's reaction is surprise at the incongruity of putting two very different concepts together. In this case the combination is of interesting artwork and simple jokes.

As you can see from the two very different examples on these pages, though, using draughtsmanship is not just about contrast. It also enables the artist to use more detail in the art to add to the humour. Randy McIllwaine's cartoon opposite requires exaggeration for his joke and the use of a full classroom scene for the reaction <u>is</u> the joke. A simpler sketch would not have worked.

Cartoonist's tip

If your drawing skills are limited you might like to try using non-drawing related effects such as collage or photo montage to illustrate your ideas and gags.

CASE STUDY

In this cartoon, Bruce Baillie takes the idea of contrasting strong illustration with a simple joke a step further. Here he is satirizing an old-fashioned drawing style. The idea of keeping pet beavers in a third floor flat is quite funny, but Bruce puts it in the context of a spoof 1930s illustration.

The illustration works by:

a) *Increasing the surprise for the viewer who is expecting to see something more traditional in the caption.*

b) *Using a spoof of an old drawing style it satirizes the mores of an earlier, more innocent age and increases the surreal notion of Bruce's idea.*

Bruce Baillie

"Of course, there are certain disadvantages to keeping pet Beavers in a 3rd. floor flat in Mayfair!" exclaimed Gurney.

Young Stephen King

Randy McIllwaine

Warning

As more work is required for larger illustration, you might like to sketch your idea first and show it to friends to check it works before you draw it up fully.

◄ *Look how Randy McIllwaine's joke about horror stories relies on exaggerated expression, while Bruce Baillie's joke is deadpan. Baillie could have justified exaggeration, but the satire of stiff upper-lip English would have been lost.*

Style workout

More polished and larger scale cartoons like the ones on these pages take more time and effort than the quick sketches discussed earlier. As the focus of the picture is generally wider, drawing skills such as a knowledge of perspective and figure drawing become more important. To improve your drawing skills try some of the following:

- If you are unfamiliar with the basics of drawing pick up a basic 'how to draw' book that will give you the ground rules.
- Practise by copying more realistic drawing styles such as *Marvel* comic-book style. Don't lose your own style, but it will add to your drawing skills.

▲ *Improve your drawing skills for illustration by doodling and sketching people and objects from real life. It will help.*

FAUX-NAIF CARTOONS

Contrasting with illustrative cartoons is the 'faux-naif' style. In cartooning this means a style that is deliberately amateur – a sort of 'I can't draw, but to Hell with it' approach. Though this style by definition suits cartoonists with less advanced drawing skills, many fine artists adopt this approach as well. Drawing 'badly' adds a humour of its own if it is done in the right way. It gives a rawness, unconventionality and immediacy to the joke that has an undefinable appeal, a little like a child's scribble.

A good drawing with a bad joke will never be funny. However, a good joke with a bad drawing can still work. You still need some skill, though. The final drawing will still have to project an 'undefinable appeal', as any helpful cartoon editor will tell you.

David Cooney

Corporate Reorganization for the Self-employed

CASE STUDY

David Cooney's work explains 'undefinable appeal' better than words. The drawing is very simple. The perspective is not quite right and the shapes, figure and face are drawn very simply, but this is part of what makes it funny. When the viewer looks at the drawing it does not feel like a professional artist making a point for the general public, but one friend talking to another. That is not to say there is no skill in the drawing, for the expression and posture of the man reflect the joke perfectly.

The comic effect here is created by:

a) *The strong observational joke. If you use this sort of drawing style, however, the jokes have to be spot on.*
b) *The wording used. The use of the word 'corporate' conjures up a large global company and contrasts perfectly with the more prosaic reality of the 'pencil cup'.*

David Myers

'Hold on – there may be a vacancy in our finance department …'

◀ *Look how David Myers hasn't even given his characters eyes or proper hands, but his visual shorthand still works owing to the strong composition of the image as a whole.*

Style workout

You would think this would be the easiest one, as the whole point is to draw in an amateur style, but as I hope I've shown from the case study, just drawing badly is not enough. If you look at the cartoon above by David Myers you can see that drawing as if you can't draw and not being able to draw are two different things. David Myers's drawing is well constructed. The perspective, balance and focus of the picture are all correct, but he has used very loose lines and shapes for his figure drawing that almost come out as a scrawl. Try to create a similar effect yourself by:

- Loosening your style. Practise drawing simple shapes such as sausages, circles and boxes quickly and sketchily.
- Avoiding heavy detail. Try to give the impression of objects without drawing them in full, such as the impression of buildings that David Myers uses for the cityscape through the window.
- Drawing up a few faces and seeing the minimum number of lines you can use to create your characters. Understated expression generally works better for this style.

▲ *If drawing isn't a strength why not try using matchstick figures? With just a few lines you can still create useful effects, as you can see from this simple sketch above.*

Applying your style

Right, now you've found a style that suits your jokes and market you still have to make the most of the jokes and 'sell' them to the viewer. Luckily this is what this section is about.

MAXIMUM EXPRESSION

Facial expression is important to cartoons as it allows the viewer to see how the characters are reacting to a given situation. Often reaction or over-reaction is necessary to indicate where the joke is or what point you are making.

Expression is the joke

As a simple example, if you are drawing someone accidentally hitting their thumb with a hammer the viewer has to understand instantly what has happened. You need to underline his pain with a strong expression and the more you exaggerate the funnier it becomes. Over-reaction to a simple or unlikely event creates humour for the reasons outlined in the section on exaggeration.

Angonoa

CASE STUDY

In Angonoa's silent cartoon *(left)* exaggerated expression is necessary for the viewer to understand the situation. A policeman talking to a man playing a video driving game would mean very little to an audience. But an obviously angry policeman talking to the same man who now looks confused and worried enables the viewer to understand the situation. Only half the humour is therefore created by the initial idea of speeding on a video game.

The rest of the comic effect is produced by:

a) The exaggerated anger of the policeman that points to the joke and is ridiculous.
b) The reaction from the driver who conveys to the viewer exaggerated fear, surprise and confusion.

Santiago Cornejo

Use exaggerated expression sparingly. If all your characters show too much reaction then you have 'raised the anti' and there is nowhere to go when you want to make a stronger point.

◄ *Santiago Cornejo's cartoon wouldn't work at all without exaggerated expression. The contrast between the first three panels and the last is the joke. Without the first panels the surprise of the last wouldn't work.*

Style workout

For the cartoonist, exaggerating the expressions of characters is one of the most fun things you can do, as you can really let your pen and imagination run riot. It is important, though, to remember to stretch your drawing in the right direction. If you want to show someone laughing heartily and you go too far they will look like they are crying or having hysterics.

So take it to the breaking point, but not beyond.

- Start by just drawing a simple expression and then keep going as far as you can without overdoing the effect.
- Remember expression is not just about facial movement. Body language helps to convey emotion too, so practise with whole figure drawing.

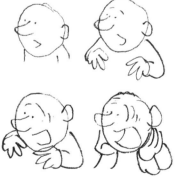

▲ *Here the position and use of hands is as integral to the result as the changes to the features.*

MINIMAL EXPRESSION

Minimal expression is a fine tool to use if your approach to humour is deadpan. It is still really a form of exaggeration, but here the cartoonist is underplaying what a normal reaction would be, rather than exaggerating it. The humour comes from the reader's surprise at a ridiculous or unlikely event being met with such a laid-back response. Cartoonists who use this style to best effect are those that seem to create their own cartoon world populated with dry, pithy figures who are surrounded by bizarre characters and events but take it all in their stride. This approach to humour seems particularly fashionable now, and is probably a reaction against the more obviously signposted jokes of the past.

'Using minimal expression is the difference between subtle humour and slapstick. If you're subtle when you present a ridiculous situation, you give the reader credit for seeing the joke for him or herself.'

Mike Baldwin

Cartoonist's tip

As there is little happening in the faces of the characters it's good to use other drawing techniques to add visual interest for the viewer. This must be done subtly or the focus will change. Marc Tyler Nobleman *(right)* uses grey shading to achieve this, while Andy McKay (Naf) *(opposite)* makes good use of black and white.

CASE STUDY

Marc Tyler Nobleman's cartoons are all populated by unflappable characters who are continually unsurprised by either their own or others' behaviour or actions. No-one laughs, shouts, shows surprise or indeed any response; they just take events as they find them. The more extreme the situation the more funny the lack of response becomes.

In this cartoon the humour comes from:

a) *The ridiculous concept that the monkey does not know that he is either adopted or a monkey.*
b) *The caption, which allows the realization to dawn on the viewer as it would the monkey.*
c) *The fact that all of this is played as if it is an everyday occurrence.*

Marc Tyler Nobleman

'Yes, you're adopted. But there's more …'

'*Stumbling across a bear is bad enough, but you're
telling me you think it knows kung-fu as well.*'

Andy McKay (Naf)

💣 **Warning**

Don't be too rigid in your style. If a character needs to show a reaction for you to get the joke across do it, but try and be subtle and keep it in tone with the rest of the cartoon.

◀ *Note in Andy McKay's (Naf's) cartoon that he still uses a downturned mouth to indicate displeasure, but it does underplay the situation the two men are in.*

Style workout

Perfecting looks of blank incomprehension isn't as hard as it sounds. Minimal expression is not the same as no expression. The cartoonist has to convey a lot with very little. Passive body language can help, but, as most expression comes from the eyes and mouth, reducing or hiding these features can create the effect you are looking for. To achieve this try some of the following:

- Making the features look more 'realistic' and in proportion. The closer they are to human proportions the more deadpan they will be in a cartoon setting.
- Alternatively, use heavy brows, glasses or noses to lessen the expression from the eyes and therefore make the character more inscrutable.
- Leaving out the mouth altogether sometimes helps.

▲ *In these examples I've achieved similar effects with different face shapes, noses, eyebrows, etc.*

MOVEMENT

Movement is essential to a lot of cartoons and is used for several different functions. Not surprisingly, it is used primarily for depicting action. In single-panel cartoons you are only really drawing one point in time, therefore you have to depict the movement in the moment which will make what is happening most clear to the viewer. This can often create humour, for the most extreme point in any movement will often be the funniest when drawn. For example, if you are drawing someone falling over, there are many points where you can catch the action, but if you use any 'frame' before the person reaches the point of no return when gravity takes over it will simply look like the person is leaning over.

Movement and body language

Movement in cartoons is not just about running, jumping, falling, etc. In fact it is probably used most often to depict exaggerated body language. As we have seen, exaggeration can add humour and as a cartoonist you will need to depict movement in your body language to heighten the effect you are trying to make. Spreading the limbs out in action or extreme gesture can help here.

Cartoonist's tip

If you are unsure about how to draw a movement practise by drawing a matchstick person first. As you are only working with simple lines it should make it easier to achieve the correct body shape and limb action before you draw the real character.

Randy McIllwaine

CASE STUDY

Randy McIllwaine shows movement in body language perfectly in this cartoon. He has a silly scenario and knows that the more extreme the reaction the sillier the scientists look and the more effective the joke will be. The reaction involves the whole body.

Here the humour is enhanced by:

a) *Exaggerating the movement by catching the most extreme part of the movement cycle.*
b) *Highlighting the movement of the whole body with expression and movement lines to give the picture a feeling of dynamism, which increases the 'drama'.*

SAY
AAARGH

John Docherty (Jorodo)

Warning

Don't try and think of a joke that specifically requires movement as it will appear forced. Use it when it will be part of a joke you have, such as Ian Baker's joke on page 32.

◀ *You don't need to have extreme expression with movement. Combining minimal expression with extreme movement can work as it increases contrast and surprise, as you can see from John Docherty's (Jorodo's) cartoon.*

Style workout

Drawing full body movement requires practice, but you can give the impression of movement quite easily by using movement lines. Movement lines are the little squiggles, lines and curves that create a mini-blur effect around the object to show where it has moved from. A circle drawn with a squiggle behind it can look like a ball travelling through the air.

Practise by:
- Drawing simple objects and different movement lines to see what effects you can get.
- Now use the same movement lines, but use them to show movement on arms, heads, bodies and legs running, jumping, etc.

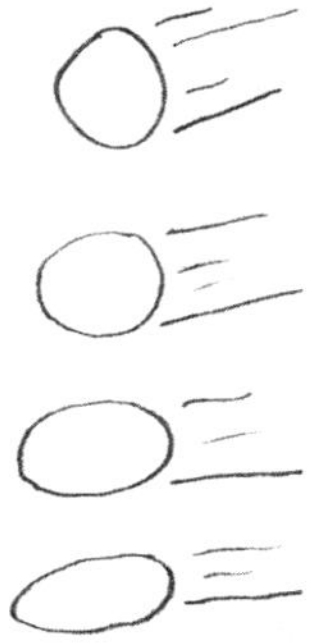

▲ *Notice how you can add movement to the ball by elongating the ball so it appears to have more energy.*

FOCUS

Focus is crucial to all cartoons. It's about drawing your cartoon in such a way that the audience instantly 'focuses' on the joke. The composition of the cartoon should be such that the reader's eye is compellingly drawn to where the action is. In most cases this is quite straightforward. As long as you keep your figures central to the action and don't use complicated backgrounds that are unnecessary, you can create simple and effective cartoons. Remember that people generally read left to right, so your cartoons should be drawn that way too. If you need to direct the 'reader' to a specific point use the eyes or body language of one of your characters as a visual sign for the viewer as to where he or she should focus.

As there are always exceptions to the basic rules have a look though the whole book to see how artists have focused their pictures in other ways. Each will use his or her particular technique.

☀ Warning

Avoid details or objects that will draw the eye away from the action. If it is prominent the viewer will assume it must be part of the joke.

Oliver Preston

Penelope sensed one of Henry's faux-pas coming on.

CASE STUDY

Oliver Preston uses a classical triangular figure composition in this cartoon to draw the viewer's eye from the man speaking up to the painting and then down to Penelope. The viewer is first drawn to the man, because with his mouth open he looks as if he is talking. The eyes then follow his up to the painting. Then, to complete the triangle, the viewer looks down. Putting the picture above its subject also helps the viewer to compare the two images quickly.

The humour relies upon:

a) *The composition of the image, as described above.*
b) *The wash shading, which further emphasizes the painting over the mantlepiece and helps the viewer to focus on the three characters as they are lighter than their background.*
c) *The deadpan expression drawn for both Penelope and her portrait.*

Stan Eales

'If there's anybody here who knows why these two should not be wed ...'

Humour can also be created by actually disguising the main element of the joke, so the viewer is surprised when he works out what is happening, and this surprise element helps the humour.

◄ *In Stan Eales' cartoon, Stan helps the humour by making the picture quite busy, and putting the sheep in the background so the viewer can be rewarded on finding him after reading the caption.*

Style workout

Picture this simple scenario, which involves two leopards. One of them is holding a tub of spot remover. The other is speaking. The caption to the cartoon reads 'Why can't you be happy with who you are?' Ask yourself the following questions before drawing up your own version of the cartoon and then compare it to Shannon Burns' original on page 88.

- Do I put the leopard talking or the one holding the tub on the left of the scene?
- Which elements are important to the joke? How do I make them obvious to the viewer?
- What detail do I need? How do I make it clear the animals are leopards? Do I need much, if any, background?

▲ *In this sketch I've kept the frame tight, made the box central, and used the eyes to direct the viewer's attention.*

SHADING AND COLOUR

Shading and colour, though not apparently funny in themselves, can be very important elements in emphasizing the humour in your work. Two functions that they perform beyond their decorative and stylistic appeal are in aiding the focus and balance of the picture (see pages 78–79) and to create atmosphere and a setting in your work, which is sometimes necessary for a joke.

Draw a quick sketch of the moon and shade round it in black or grey. Notice how the eye is drawn to the area of white that is the moon, not to the surrounding black. We naturally look to a lighter area in a picture, because it acts like a spotlight to focus our attention.

Shading and colour also serve to create the mood in a work. If your joke requires a sunny, gloomy or frightening scene as part of the joke, then colour, wash or pen shading can help the effect. This is also a chance to display your own artistic strengths.

Warning

Don't dismiss the decorative and stylistic importance of shading, etc. Art editors sometimes need it to enhance the look of their publication.

CASE STUDY

Oliver Preston's cartoon shows wash shading used for focus and atmosphere. The use of a very dark grey wash contrasts with the lighter areas to lift them and focus the viewer on the faces and the figures. What is more important is that the same dark wash gives the whole picture a dark, ominous Gothic feel. This sinister look is actually part of the joke and the viewer needs to feel the sense of foreboding of the bereaved.

What makes this cartoon work is:

a) The initial idea that undertakers might have an alternative 'disposal' method. This appeals to a taste for black humour. It relies on our need to laugh at the things that frighten us.

b) The wash, which provides the disturbing element for the black humour, but the picture still needs to be friendly and warm, or the viewer really would be 'frightened' and the joke would disappear.

Oliver Preston

'Cremation or burial or would he prefer a surprise?'

Mike Williams

'… fourth floor … white goods … garden furniture … alternative medicine …'

Colour use

Most colour work is commissioned and used for specific features in publications, greeting cards, etc. and is not used that regularly for single-panel cartoons. When it is used, however, colour is rarely just decorative. Stronger colours and white can be used to signpost the action and create atmosphere in a cartoon. For example, yellows can add a happy feel, reds can highlight danger, etc.

◀ Mike Williams has used a dark tone for the area around the lift to frame it and draw the viewer towards what's inside. The area outside the frame is used to give context, so we know it's a lift.

Cartoonist's tip

As you can't 'draw' sunlight you can create the impression of it by strong shadows and shading. Even light shading can give the impression of a hot day if the sun is also there to give a visual clue.

Style workout

Look at Mike Williams' cartoon above. It was originally created in colour. Create a black and white line-drawing version of the picture yourself. Then make some photocopies and experiment with different types of pen shading, wash and colour. How would you use shading and colour to highlight the witchdoctor at the back of the lift and the liftman who is speaking? Try some of these:

- Use crosshatch shading, pen shading and solid black to darken the unimportant areas, leaving white in the important ones you want to focus on.
- Use full colour, but use light hues and tones for the unimportant areas within the lift, and put in stronger ones for the mask and lift attendant.

▲ In my version I've used loose crosshatching to darken the scene, but I've left the mask white so that it is highlighted.

SCALE

In Section One on pages 31–33 I explained how exaggeration could be used to create humour by taking concepts and stretching them to their limits. Scale is the term I use to take the same principle and use it to create humour in the artwork itself. Scale is about exaggerating and expanding the scene or detail of a picture for humorous effect.

Look at Mike Williams' cartoon opposite. The increased scale and broader canvas enhances or even creates the humour. If you've seen Monty Python's film *The Life of Brian* you may remember the scene where Brian opens a window naked to find a crowd of thousands outside. This huge crowd is integral to the joke as it magnifies his embarrassment to the point of ridiculousness. In Mike's cartoon we laugh not just at the notion of a lifeboat rescuing Noah's animals, but the scale at which it is depicted. It's the crowd scene that makes the joke. Would it be as funny if there were fewer animals in the boat?

Detail

Exaggerating the 'scale' of detail can create the same effect. The concept of the joke does not change, but stretching the artwork to the point of ridiculousness can make the joke, as we can see below.

> *'I love using lots of detail and a large canvas for my work but remember that the joke still comes first. Try not to clutter the cartoon with too much detail at the joke's expense.'*
>
> Oliver Preston

"DAD, THIS IS BRET. . .BRET, THIS IS DAD ."

CASE STUDY

In Stefano Baratti's cartoon the joke is not really about costume as such, but about social prejudice and embarrassment. Stefano is commenting on being gay/camp and people's/parents reaction to it, but it couldn't work without the drawing.

The scene is funny because:

a) The magnificent detail and exaggeration of Bret's costume magnifies the tension of the situation and contrasts with the conservative parent.

b) The expressions clearly signpost the nature of the situation for the viewer and allow them to squirm with embarrassment for all concerned.

Mike Williams

Cartoonist's tip

Crowd scenes are a time-consuming business. Try just drawing the first row of faces and then give the impression of heads and faces behind by drawing simple shapes.

◀ *Look how Mike Williams uses animals that will provide most comic effect and be clearly seen in a big crowd. The angry sea also helps as it heightens the comic pathos of the scene.*

Style workout

Look again at Stefano Baratti's cartoon opposite. Though he has used exaggerated detail the whole scenario is still within the limits of credibility. If you are going to draw an extravagant crowd scene or some 'enhanced' detail there are still boundaries to bear in mind. If the viewer is concentrating more on one aspect of a picture than the picture as a whole then you won't be able to get the idea behind it across.

Redraw Stefano's cartoon in your own style, but try to:
• Stretch the costume idea even further. Keep going until it dominates so much that the original idea disappears.
• Now reduce the exaggeration of the costume until it becomes so boring that, again, the joke doesn't make sense.

▲ *In my version the costume dominates too much and becomes the joke. The social comedy is lost.*

WHAT WENT WRONG

You'll be pleased to hear that even professionals don't get it right all the time. In these two pages I've included a couple of extreme examples of cartoons that I've done that haven't worked at all that I hope will be instructive.

Bad idea and bad drawing

My initial thought for the joke below was to have a pun based on instant coffee and Lottery Instant scratch cards. I thought the stupid idea of someone scratching a jar of instant coffee with a coin as if it was a scratch card would be funny. It wasn't, because nobody understood the joke. The pun was too obscure and the drawing incomprehensible. There are no visual clues for the viewer that I was comparing instant coffee to Lottery Instants and the action of the figure doesn't look like a man scratching with a coin. Perhaps if I'd set the scene in a newsagent's next to a Lottery Instant display it might have worked, as the viewer would have seen the parallel I was making. However, it was such a weak idea that I decided it wasn't worth the time redrawing it.

> 'What works in your head doesn't always work on paper, but often your first idea is the best. I've often tried to improve on a gag, but always come back to my first thought.'
>
> *Clive Goddard*

 Warning

Don't be too self-critical. Sometimes cartoonists are not the best judges of their own work. A cartoon you love may never sell, but a bad pun that you submit as a 'filler' to the rest of a batch might do very well.

▶ *The failure of this cartoon demonstrates that context is the key to successful cartoons. If the man was holding a scratch card our brains would assume he was holding a coin. As he isn't, they don't.*

INSTANT COFFEE

Just bad drawing

There was no problem with the joke in this cartoon. The magazine I submitted it to wanted it, but there were mistakes within the artwork. They sent it back to me, and asked for changes. The obvious mistake was the spelling, and that could be easily fixed (though it was embarrassing and should have been avoided).

The real problem was that when they reduced it to the size it would appear in print the wording was hard to read and the thin lines I'd used began to disappear. I had to redraw the whole cartoon using a thicker line and making the text more legible for the reduction.

The moral of this tale is to always check the size at which your finished artwork will appear and make sure that your drawing will be viewable at that size, with good line quality and correct wording.

◀ *Look on the first version (left) how the poor line quality has meant that the eye and the mouth have disappeared, the background is incomplete and the writing hard to read when reduced. A thicker pen solved all these problems (below left at full-drawn size and right at final printed size).*

The art of captioning

Having a funny idea and being able to draw it are all well and good, but unless you can find the right wording for the caption the whole joke can be lost.

Captioning is a skill in itself. There are two particular requirements. One is the ability to get your point over in the clearest (often the most concise) way. The other is to use words that in themselves the audience will be amused by. You won't always use both skills on the same cartoon, but you need to be aware of both.

> 'Sometimes when inspiration fails me, I look through a dictionary searching for a funny word, and try and create a cartoon around that.'
>
> Ian Baker

Cartoonist's tip

Some words are just 'funny'. I couldn't tell you why. 'Turnip' is a funny word. 'Table' is not. When appropriate try to use words that you find funny. If you find a word funny there is a good chance someone else will too.

CASE STUDY

For most cartoons less is more, but this Duncan McCoshan (Knife) cartoon (where verbosity is the joke) is a fine example of how language can be funny in itself. A long explanatory sentence would normally be dull to read, but Duncan's skill is his use of language and turn of phrase.

Here the comic effect is created by:

a) Choosing phrases such as 'prevailing easterly wind' that seem funny in themselves.
b) The verbose and pompous sound of the words. Duncan could simply have used the phrase 'wind in the east'.

Duncan McCoshan 'Knife'

'It's a vital approach shot. I'd use a seven iron and try and hook it into the prevailing easterly wind and hope to drop it above the pin because it's a pretty fast green and there's that big sand trap to the front left. But you'll probably just belt it straight into the trees as usual.'

Anthony Kelly

'You're going on a very short journey.'

Less is more

The viewer generally expects to grasp the joke and enjoy laughing or smiling in just a few seconds. If there is a lot of text to read, and it takes a while to digest that, the immediacy of the joke can be lost. As a cartoonist you will want to use as few words as possible to get your point across. As we have seen previously, there are exceptions to this, but, by and large, less is more.

Look at Anthony Kelly's cartoon above. The temptation, once you have the idea and need to find the wording for it, is to use more words than you actually need, because you forget the picture tells most of the story. If I created this joke I might have started with the caption 'I predict that you're going on a very short journey', but the prediction is evident in the picture anyway, so the wording can be cut right back so that the effect is more pithy.

◀ *Look at the number of visual clues Anthony Kelly uses to reduce the wording required. The sign, headscarf and tablecloth all reduce the need for extra words.*

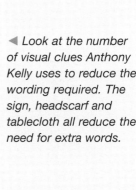 **Warning**

Without the visual clue of the symbol on the dummy's head in the cartoon on this page, we wouldn't know it was a crash-test dummy, and the caption would have to start with the phrase 'Well, Mr Crash Test Dummy …'. The more visual clues you put in the picture, the less wording you will need. Remember the cliché that a picture is worth a thousand words?

▶ *Most captions in single-panel cartoons are speech. In Robert Thompson's cartoon the wording reflects natural speech patterns. Don't write 'do not' when you would say 'don't'.*

'I don't like the look of this.'

Editing your caption

To achieve the most concise wording you can, here is a tip I gained from fellow cartoonist John Byrne. He suggests you write down the caption as you first think of it and then spend time crossing out all those words that are not absolutely essential to the meaning. In a very basic example, instead of writing 'Would you pass me the salt please,' all you really need is 'pass the salt'. Humour can be created by the wording itself, but the caption should also facilitate quick understanding, and not get in the way. I see a lot of very funny ideas from non-English-speaking cartoonists. However, as English is not their first language, they don't always put in all the grammar, idioms, etc. that make the caption seem natural. In these cases, however funny the idea may be, the joke vanishes as I stumble over errors, or have to reread to understand.

◀ *By having as much visual information as possible Shannon Burns avoids a more clumsy caption, which might start 'Leopards don't need spot remover – why can't you …'.*

'Why can't you be happy with who you are?'

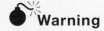
Dan Rosandich

◀ *Though it is conventional to have the wording separate from the artwork, you can add it to speech bubbles if you like, as can be seen in this cartoon by the American cartoonist Dan Rosandich.*

Caption workout

The best way to perfect your captions, as I mentioned on page 88 is to practise editing down your wording and letting the picture speak for itself. Of course, you can sometimes create humour by breaking the convention, as with Duncan McCoshan's cartoon on page 86, but let's get the ground rules right first. Look at the following sentences and remove all the words that you think are unnecessary.

- 'I don't know about you, but I'd prefer the lasagne.'
- 'Why can't you be more like your friend Peter? He's a corporate lawyer.'
- 'Okay Simpkins. I know it's Christmas, but do we really need the turkey now?'

Just for fun – now try and think of some images that would match these random phrases.

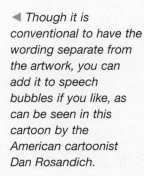
Warning

If you are going to put the caption in the artwork, the writing should be clear and easy to read. Don't just use standard handwriting, but develop a lettering style.

CARTOON SHOWCASE

Here are a few great cartoons showing a range of styles and humour. Having read the book you should now have mastered the tools to create some of your own.

'So which of you stays at home looking after the kids all day?'

I love the Grizelda cartoon above because it's so visual. The joke relies on Grizelda's graphic ability to convey the mother's stress in an exaggerated and comic way, using concise, but very expressive, linework. This instant visual understanding allows the punch line to work. This is the perfect example of the saying that 'a picture tells a thousand words'. If you tried to explain this concept in words it would be very long, and not very funny.

Ham Khan

Above: The joy of Ham Khan's work is his apparently simple, but actually very skilled, line drawing. The line seems to flow to create the characters, and has an appeal of its own. This stylized approach creates a more sophisticated edge to the humour that adds to the whole effect.

Below: Michael Ryan's (Moic's) cartoon is one of those jokes that everyone loves. Not all gags will appeal to all people but this one must come close. Its instant appeal relies less on the style in which it is drawn and more on the focus of the picture for an instant comic hit.

Isabella Bannerman

ACTUAL EXTENT OF DOUG'S OFF-ROAD ADVENTURES.
(SEE BOX FOR DETAIL)

This is a wonderful piece of observation by Isabella Bannerman, which she has turned into a fine cartoon. Everyone will recognize the phenomenon of fashionable city dwellers buying off-road vehicles that never see the countryside. It's a funny concept in itself because it exemplifies how silly some fashions can be. Bannerman's gentle ridicule here, though, is particularly effective because she depicts the notion by exaggerating the concept to the most ridiculous extreme to get the point across.

Robert Thompson

Above: Many jokes are drawn around puns, but not all of them work. This cartoonist, Robert Thompson, however, is a master of the pun. His skill is to create obscure puns that no one else would think of and then to create unusual and silly scenarios.

Left: Artist Mike Baldwin has created a style where his characters live in a world of childish naivety. Their faces often make us smile before we've even read the joke. This one makes us laugh because his 'children' are doing something incongruously childish, in what should be a dangerous situation.

Paul Black (Fishhead)

The cartoon above may create quite a bit of 'friendly' debate. I think this is an 'I love it or hate it' cartoon. Paul Black (Fishhead) has a drawing and humour style that are very 'left field'. The drawing is stylized and the dot shading adds an unusual texture to his work, which complements the 'mad' text. I've selected this one because his fresh approach to drawing and humour contrast so well with the more traditional approach.

Richard Jolley

'Yep, that was one serious paper cut.'

Above: There is something funny about pirates bragging at a bar even before reading the unexpected and silly brag. Cartoons often have more than one element that provides humour. Richard Jolley's choice of pirates as the subject of this joke is as important as the paper cut concept itself.

Below: Expression is the key to me in one of my favourite cartoons by Duncan McCoshan (Knife). Duncan has captured something in the face of the cat that all cat lovers will understand. It's actually a remarkably surreal image, but the expression makes the cat's behaviour seem totally believable.

" THE CAT'S BEEN AT THE CLASSICS AGAIN"

Selling your cartoons

As a cartoon fan you will have seen cartoons in a whole range of media. These are all potential markets for your work too. They include newspapers, consumer and trade magazines, books, ads, the web and greetings cards.

Selling 'on spec'

Some magazines and newspapers in the UK such as *Private Eye*, the *Sun* and *The Spectator* publish cartoons submitted to them on spec. This means that artists have sent them cartoons speculatively, knowing that they take cartoons, but obviously they have no guarantee that the editor will use their work. This open policy means if your work is good enough you can get published in recognized publications. Needless to say this is harder than it sounds, and you must be prepared for a lot of rejection, but if your work is good and you keep sending to them, they could well publish your cartoons.

Getting a regular spot

Many consumer magazines, trade publications and newspapers already have, or might be willing to consider, a regular cartoon feature. However, they will only take work that reflects the readership they cater for. Getting a regular spot involves marketing your work by putting a package together of relevant work they will like and pitching your cartoons as a feature for their readers. There are a lot of publications on the newsstands catering for many diverse interests, so half the battle is selecting good potential targets. You don't want to waste time with magazines who will never use cartoons, or have no budget for cartoons. Always make a quick phone call first to find out if they are interested in taking cartoons and, if so, find the right person they should be sent to.

Be professional

When sending off samples of your work for a regular spot or on spec you should always be professional in your approach. Include a short businesslike covering letter with your contact details and a few relevant samples of your work. If you are pitching for a regular spot draw up a few samples to explain the feature. If you are submitting on spec include about ten drawings that you hope will appeal. Editors are busy people, so don't write pages of explanatory notes or package your cartoons in such a way that they are hard to view quickly.

Market yourself

Beyond direct contact to publications there are other ways to get yourself noticed by people who are actually searching for cartoonists. Advertising agencies, designers, publishers and businesses often need to commission work. Some cartoonists have their own website, or advertise in the advertising and design industry trade press. However, this can be expensive and may not produce results. Joining an agency, syndicate or stock house can reduce your initial outlay, but remember that they will take a percentage of your fees, and they will often only take on established artists. You'll probably have to demonstrate that you've been able to sell your work yourself before an agent will be prepared to take you on.